ROADS
BOOK 1

Ina Schroders-Zeeders

Winter Goose
Publishing

Winter Goose Publishing
2701 Del Paso Road, 130-92
Sacramento, CA 95835

www.wintergoosepublishing.com
Contact Information: info@wintergoosepublishing.com

Roads Book 1

COPYRIGHT © 2015 by Ina Schroders-Zeeders

First Edition, March 2015

Cover Art by Winter Goose Publishing
Cover Art Picture by David Agnew
Typeset by Odyssey Books

ISBN: 978-1-941058-27-5

Published in the United States of America

To my husband, Toussaint Schroders

Contents

I

The Road to the Other

What We Share

Between the common features we share
and our uniqueness is no border;
I find you differently in any order of my mind.
There is no box in which to place you
though I'm aware you and I are much alike.

I saw you sip your coffee carefully as I sipped mine.
Like me, too often did you burn yourself in eagerness.
Between the common features that we share—a frown, a line—
is what I know so well of you and maybe you of me.
It's there we might continue our voyage to each other.

Ending and Beginning

The best books don't have a happy ending, you said.
Even after you cut out the last wine-soaked pages
of Anna Karenina it still was a good book so we both thought,
misery reads well and your voice was a good voice
for reading about sadness.
That night our child was born.

I heard the rain when you read a poem to me
and the sound, your timbre, my eyes closed, meant
life, an ordinary day was lying ahead, not ending soon.
You made it special. This is what matters, so I know now.
For this we began the journey together.
I think she jumped in front of a train.

Pink Petals

The scent of pink petals is hanging in the room:
with my eyes closed I'm with you in that flower shop,
years ago but the flowers smell the same as then,
to get something nice but cheap for a funeral—
we didn't really know the deceased very well
who was in his eighties when he died in his sleep,
we only knew that he liked flowers very much.

We ended up spending our money on roses
and on those flowers we didn't know what to call.
We almost forgot to dress in black. The graveyard
never smelt so grand and fine that I remember.
Memories last longer than flowers in water.
Forever: a kind old man behind his window,
waving, when I smell those pink flowers in the room.

I Love You

Another line you said that puzzles me,
its meaning lost in laughter and your wink,
it should be written in the bluest ink,
a phrase so beautiful, it cannot be.

Your kindness flows in such abundancy,
the sentences you whisper always link
to what you mean to me, but what to think
of how you act, that seems to disagree?

The words you tell me: I shall take them light,
not much expecting, as they seem too good
for truth, and you are such a lie, you are.

I don't believe that you will stay all night,
but let this knowledge not ruin the mood:
the best in love is you, the best by far.

Short Memories

Evanescent thoughts of you while I write
(memories too short to be called as such)
make me open a window, all windows
so I can smell tar from the ships,
then you appear swiftly in my lines
as you and tar, the smell of it are one,
my words can only write this palimpsest
as past has found this way to last in me
and windows batter memories of you.

Justification

Trees die for the sake of poetry,
some were homes to nightingales—
one should be able to tell
by the poems on their paper.

Flowers are cut with the sharpest knives
to be given away affectionately,
but often the roses
die for nothing.

Words are read, silently tasted for sound,
their meanings unheard,
drifting through air
into oblivion.

The nightingale loses its home,
the flower its life, and words their voice
to connect one searching heart
to another waiting soul.

The Stranger

This happened long ago when I, still young,
did not belief in angels (nor in hell),
nothing was biblical that I could tell
but life would change, and I should bite my tongue.

The stranger in our local place-to-be
wore white and made the dusty sunlight twirl,
his eyes were looking for just any girl
and out of all the ones, this man chose me.

We smiled of course and then he took my hand.
We danced a bit and drank a beer or two.
He didn't talk much, strangers never do.
We walked all night over the moonlit strand.

He showed me what I should have seen before,
the stars in patterns they had never been.
He offered me his shoulder then to lean,
the sea began to sing, could I need more?

He took the ferry, to leave at seven.
I never saw him back, don't know his name
nor what his business was, for what he came.
I only know that he was sent from heaven.

The New Girl

We stood before the open gate
and waited in the springtime sun
as none of us spoke much that time,
we only heard the wind blow hard.

We watched her get her red kite up:
the girl who came from Amsterdam.
Her hair was black in curls and shone,
she wore a jacket and a scarf.

She let the kite go in the air
and you ran forward through the gate
to grab the line. You saved the day.
You took her hand. We held our breath.

We, others, knew right there and then
that you may never let her go,
so obvious it was to us.
The kite is gone, but love has stayed.

Your children now play in the grass,
a girl with black and curly hair,
the boy's is red just like his dad,
and they have kites that fly all day.

Bus Trip

We stand too close
breathing our mutual breaths.
The road is meandering,
I feel your skin.

We hold on nicely,
swaying by every turn.
The bus is crowded
in hot summer landscape.

Stopped: passengers are leaving,
your body invites mine.
You step out last.
The door shuts again.

Seats enough, I stand,
see your lifting hand,
my journey already over,
destiny reached in your eyes.

The Wise Lover

You speak of life in invisible glyphs,
had I known you longer I might grasp you,
for now I take every scene for granted,
cerulean curtains behind you in waft.

Each day you find a treasure in poems.
I watch your skin against cyan-blue cloth.
Without a doubt you will leave me sooner
and I shall wear blue for a while till fall.

Messengers

So many birds came by my side, near to the sea,
and every one took just one thought, one sigh of me.
As feathers ruffled over me, they promised to
bring all my greetings, take my everlasting love to you.

So there they went, they soon flew out of sight.
If one has reached its destination, might
it be the black gull with the last thought I have sent,
because of all the thoughts, it is the dearest one that went.

Sex

Completely
overwhelmed by you;
not moving.
You caress.
Holding my breath, I taste you,
let you enter me.

We are one,
you lead the moving.
Skin on skin.
Deep inside
you are a stranger no more.
We have lost ourselves.

Before We Meet

Just leaning on your shoulder I'll be fine,
the dusty sunlight colouring our hair,
I am so hoping you will cross that line,
move further on and show me that you care.
It is your presence I'll be so aware,
I cannot see myself just leave you here,
though leaning on your shoulder I won't dare,
I have no clue of what it is I fear
or how I should behave when you appear.
No words come to my rescue now I need
to keep my cool, I know that you are near,
and all I think of is to do the deed.
I'm dreading every second of our meet!

Be Coming

How to call?
You looked for a word
naming me,
just a word
describing your emotions
(but I'm no beauty).

Becoming:
you tasted this word,
syllables,
before use,
their sound sweet sparkles in spring,
then became my love.

You giggled,
watched the curtains dance,
lavender
heavy scent,
we stayed in the sunlit bed,
good days of silence.

Figurative Sense

We were both students then,
you the best in grammar,
teaching me a lot;
me too eager to learn.

After a few lessons
we fell in love perhaps,
(you said so, I felt I
owed you in return).

"Love can grow," so you said,
"to a much larger state,
if you let nature be,
if you start love afresh."

Then you took me upstairs
where proudly you showed me
what a metaphor is
well expressed in the flesh.

Detective

How lonely must you have been, first owner
of this second-hand detective, a "Maigret,"
written in French by Georges Simenon,
the pages almost brown of age,
not turned nor touched for forty years or on.

You left some items in the book, as marks:
a serrated photo, black and white,
shows a young man smoking a pipe in rain,
on the flip side it just says: "c'est moi,"
and a note, hastily written, with a stain.

It is not much to reconstruct your past,
the handwriting is girlish, round and broad,
she must have led you on, but when and how,
who knows? You never sent the photo, right?
The note just said: "I cannot make it now."

Apocalypse When?

One of these days the world will come to end,
it is not certain what will happen then,
no matter if you practise church or zen,
we probably shall die, it may depend.

One of these days we'll know where dead folk went,
a concept, new to every kind of man,
Apocalypse will come, no one knows when,
but soon they say, are you afraid my friend?

The world will always be, I do not care
what others say, as they just have no clue
and if that time has come, well we shall see.

One of these days ahead we must go there,
and walk the route the way all people do,
to find there's more for us, and all be free.

Dove

Our friendship meant we played with dolls,
skipping rope and swimming in cold water.
We saw a dove come out its egg, a birth,
then watched your brother kill it moments later.

One summer night you told me about life,
that pigeons always know the long way home,
that mothers want their sons no matter what
but daughters must deserve their parents' love.

It didn't make much sense to me that night
but I did know your family well enough,
and it was true perhaps for every girl,
we should find out. As how were we to know.

Sometimes your father threw the family out,
for days you would not come to school
until you did show up again once more
so angry, full of hate. With other friends.

You often left to be alone elsewhere,
it never meant you didn't want to go,
as staying was no option in those days.
You are that dove to me in many ways.

Schooldays

In the café with no music
where the presumed mute barman worked,
there used to be a silence
in between your thoughts and mine,
a secret universe where we could meet.

As you made one of those thin cigarettes your ally
and smoke would curl upon the yellow sooted wall,
the contours of your face were fading in the grey.

Only a street away from school
was the place where all was possible
but nothing happened.
Your hand was close to mine,
you could have reached.

Remember how the barman stood as always,
his neck seemed broken
as he dried his glasses with that cloth,
the sunbeams with the dancing dust,
us dancing without touching without music
but the beating of our hearts so every move
was moving us apart some more.

The barman smiled and sunshine made him like an angel.
He didn't hear the silent conversation that went on.
It used to be a place where we would be in silence between
classes.

Out of the café's window we could watch the birds fly free
across the graveyard over the old stones,
where no one lied that we would know,
we didn't need much more at all.

This place, not ours, was our shelter
from painful foolish loudness, laughter.

We sat in rain outside during our lunch together
or helped the barman do the dishes, and this was so enough.
Some moments after we had left one day,
the barman screamed out loud.
He fell while we were inside school. The postman was his
witness.

We came to know. His death, which was the end of our silence,
although we did not know him well, meant that we had no
choice but talk.
As if a rope had broken, something snapped and let all go,
we had to speak of him awhile,
and of much more, we cried the rainy day that he was buried,
when we realised no people came to see him off.

We hardly knew his name but how we knew his voice.
And now his scream, that we had missed by seconds,
came standing there between us as the reaper,
the dust still dancing in the sunlight.

The café was no longer our hiding place from noise. It closed.
Sometimes I see your face in smoke
or hear your heart in silence.

Curfewed Summer of '74

Like an unnecessary metaphor
not adding anything to our encounter,
the evening came each time,
uninvited and too early
in a long, black dress so tight,
with too much lace and glitter.
Her lipstick was the shade of dusk
already fading, her eyes were cold and bitter.
She came first, her lazy spouse the night
approached us slowly with the hour.
We couldn't stay together, in the presence
of this unkind pair. He was the worst.
We had so much to tell each other,
but she was here now and she hated us.
She yawned and grinned a lot.
We shivered in the shadow of her cold
while we ignored her.
It never helped, she would not go.
Reluctantly we parted then at last.
The day had gone too soon,
as we were well aware. And eight dark hours
she and night would be dancing on our floor.
But when daylight came,
night ran away and we could meet once more.

Pen Pals

From less than acquaintances to more
we dwelled between paper walls,
words whispering in every letter:
this is how our hearts met,
honest and curious, revealing through ink,
bit by bit, in envelopes crossing the sea.

The start of you and me,
before the adventure
became that of a meeting in the flesh.
The we began handwritten, always sealed
with a closing kiss, stamped in silence
and carried to the mailbox through the rain.

The Swan

A swan you are, the way you curve,
obnoxious though in your desire,
your wings burn red in morning fire as we
touch the other one in turn. The sunset
is the first thing that we see,
watching it together as it rises
out of the waves, new light to be,
embedding both of us with care
as promise for a future we don't have.

Over the water your wings are spread,
your body now an arc above me,
sheltered from the world, from cold,
our sacred place, your voice,
that of a priest, seems old
and calm, and echoes in the temple,
over and over you say my name. I'm told
a swan again you'll leave me
when I'm sleeping after dream.

After Lace and Silver Days

The lace and silver days are over,
the rough wood is the floor of our dinners now
but the candles still wave their shades
in wild imagination
over the old walls
of our humble fortress in the village,
and your voice is deeper.
Your quick smiles
tell me your thoughts
are those of when we first met.
We do not need the lace and silver
to taste the richness of the food,
to feel each other's memory
and be lovers in the iron bed,
to hear the lark sing just for us.

Leaving France

Your words became dust
blowing over the land
finding sea. Fading,
life seemed at its best,
in the grey of Normandy,
as was the smell of dying flowers.

The breeze brings whispers
of our time together, while memories
linger over lavender fields.
Now the cliffs of France
are disappearing, as is
the smell of her blossom.

I shall look for your words
wherever I go, in every smile
will be reflexions of our days,
memories of blooming fields
and how we ran through the colours
and how we were one with the world.

Pause

Now, halfway on your journey, have a pause,
the days have lost all light and go on blind,
except for somewhere in the morning when
the low sun gives away a sample beam,
before returning under cotton clouds

to hibernate some more and dream of spring,
see all of this before the darkness comes
before you walk on further down the road.

Sharing the First Light

Someone distant to share
the first light of morning,
dust dancing in sunbeams.
After a night of feeling alone,
to find saved in a message,
your words, returning and lingering
to give this day meaning.
Someone to share
just about everything.

Screaming in Cadence

I took in everything I saw
with force, as never to forget
that moment on the platform
in erasing snow: the coats around us,
the red wool of the scarfs,
and the damping breath.

You went lost on the crowded platform,
before you could give me the red roses,
I waved without seeing you,
it was goodbye forever
without a real ending.

Sometimes you know that tragedy
is happening under your eyes.
In dying winter light,
in sounds and movement
of the leaving train it was apparent
that you were on your way,
never returning.

We had not said it
but we felt it just the same.
Already out of touch you said my name,
the sound fell screaming on the rails.

When all was quiet,
the setting sun was burning
and you were gone forever.
Alone, the crowd now gone
I walked away in the opposite direction.

When I looked back,
I noticed a rose lying on the rails.
Had you thrown it out of the window?

It got crushed by already another train,
the red confetti making blood stains in the sky.
By then your train had slowly faded in cadence:
Goodbye, goodbye, goodbye.

Found

Finding without searching,
a few old books you left me
in which you dried
the flowers that we picked.
They died between the pages,
every fragile petal
becoming dust and rot,
as I find that you loved me,
that you have loved me not.

Your Voice

Your voice does things for me, like colours do,
a bright red on a sort of turquoise blue,
your sentences surprising to my mind.

I like to dream away with just that voice,
and think: could there have been a better choice,
should I have waited, till you knew to find?

I cannot say I am not happy now,
I try to live the best way I know how,
without your voice but in my memory.

Sometimes I think I hear your laugh somewhere,
it's only in my mind. I am aware
that I'm alone when you are not with me.

Sisyphus

Sisyphus kept trying but how many times
he tried to move the rock up on the hill.
"I am the man who moved the stone,
I know my goal, my effort may be so in vain
but I am trying for your love," you said comparing.

Your time on Earth was penalty and fall;
my times with you are more mundane in café meetings,
in whispers sepia and silence.
All I carry with me from our love
are lies so heavily a burden on my shoulders:

such burdens, atrocities and more, but always
I found you back again, your touch. My Sisyphus.
I keep the rocks that you have moved in secret boxes.
They are what matters to me most,
what holds and carries on my shoulders.

What more would love be anyway:
the necklace captures all of me,
you don't weigh much in memory,
and I'll await you up there, when
finally you're there to meet me on the hill.

Smashing

Loving you
was like smashing a piggy jar
to find just enough money
for a new piggy jar.
But the smashing was priceless.

Leaving you
was like taking a wellness bath
with a bar of purest soap:
no itchy rash after
but with no foam nor scent to enjoy.

Incomparable

Now autumn leaves are twirling, restless ghosts
reminding me with sizzling whispers of the afterlife
of summer days, I won't compare our love as such.
After death, more beautiful the leaf lies in the mud.
I won't compare our love to a dead tree leaf though.

Decay is in the air, the rot sets in. More beautiful
the leaf becomes. Till all is gone, I watch each day.
I can't compare our love to a dead tree leaf in the mud.
Next spring the Maple will be green again; for us,
there won't be new leaves on the uprooted tree.

Children

We only spoke as reassurance
that the other was not sleeping,
or dead even, and how to tell the difference,
while around us all was dark, and silent
between the lighthouse beams above us.
We sat under a cobalt sky so far away
in time from any bold romantic thought,
yet there was silver in the moon, and it was huge.
I remember your reaching for my hand
after we heard a sudden owl's *oohoo*.
Our feet were dangling over water
as we sat there on the landing,
all the universe around us
we felt sheltered pointing at the stars
and we watched a ship sail in the moonlight.
I won't forget, such magic
was there in the air for both of us,
as we had slipped out of our houses,
that warm and silent summer night,
alone the two of us when we were five and six.

Cold

Now even your dog won't know me
when we pass in the street—
but how she loved me as a puppy.
I see her aging body stroll
with pain, deformed slow steps.

One day she's gonna bite me surely
if I try to pad her on the back.
It must mean something
that it means more to me
what the dog thinks than what you think.
Cold is in your Lassie's eyes
and it's the heat of summer.

Heat

On first glimpse the shiver was that of a fever maybe,
but the tears you brought in my eyes
had nothing to do with my body's condition:
you moved me. You supposed I was in heat,
so I let you make all the ritual manoeuvres
to get us laid, to fornicate, to pretend love.

As for lust you were a train and I a tunnel,
you a steaming plough and I was earth.
The point in all of this? I had no idea during.
The train went to an unknown destiny,
the seed, looking for some fertile soil,
every little polliwog a possible new person,
fell pointless on the concrete of the diaphragm.

Soon after you left, the tunnel imploded,
the earth became a desert where tumbleweed rolled.

After Heat

After sex, in a halo of understanding,
we walked hand in hand
sharing warmth through our skins.
The cold air coming from the platform
made you put on your mittens.

My hand, the first to know
it was already over before it had started,
became the last part of my body
that you saw,
waving all of it away.

Overnight Issue

The issue was living in the house
standing between us,
hanging on the couch,
lying in our bed,
here to stay for at least a week.
We had not spoken since the issue came
with all its vintage luggage,
unpacking more and more old pain.

By every sound that entered from the street
there was relief, the bitter silence
broken for a moment. The issue groaned.
After some days its shape got rounder,
more compact giving room

for harsh politeness.
For conversation without fun.
For passing butter and deciding on a shopping list.

Finally an eyeful sadness and a hug
was all we used to chase the issue out.
We made it leave the bedroom first,
then down the stairs it went.
It only left some minor items
in the house to linger on.
Standing in the door,
the issue turned its head to start again
but we gave it the finger.

Vagaries

I stare rudely over coffee in your face
now vagaries have come across.
Anything can happen in this place,
between a blink and reasoning
is room for gain or loss.

The café is about to close.
Staring rudely over coffee,
pondering my odds, my chances,
I didn't notice that you rose and left.
You never even noticed me. I feel bereft.

Heads or Tails

I watch how you still ponder during the flipping;
heads up or under, there is no telling
how the rolling coin may fall, nor where exactly.
It's landing on the edge. Now what?
Why wait at all to go away?

The die has now been cast. It does not matter
how the coin falls or how dice roll, what I feel.
Though the penny is still rolling,
no heads nor tails are making up our minds
with the blinking coin forever spinning.

This is the last game that we play.
The coin rolls on, we let it pass
out of our sight under the skirting.
Decisions have been made without its say.
'Twas heads. I am so sure it was.

Walking Through Poems

I walk through all your poems as I gasp for air.
I'm much aware this is the voyage of my life
and corridors of spoken green surround me going there.

I feel the whispers that you blow over my face as balm,
soft vales of pinkish lace embracing me.
You speak and smile in verse, you talk of love.

Then such romantic issues float beside us as we walk
to be the buoys for every mile we go across this sea,
so indigo and longing that it makes me weak.

This way I don't know who you are at all. I seek
the meaning of the whispers that you blow over my face.
All yours I walk through poems and I gasp for air.

Heaven's Kindness

More of such moments would mean love,
we both can't handle that right now
so this must be the end, you say.
You get your winter coat and put it on.

You walk away to catch your train
and there I go as well to be with you a little longer,
for one more of such moments as if I have not had enough.
The rain pours sadness over our shoulders.

I find your hand, still warm, familiar, squeeze it,
this letting go seems like the making of another moment.
You slip out of my touch and I of yours
as trains don't wait for minds to change.

More of such moments would mean love, you said.
So this must be the end. We both can't handle more.
The rain is all that's left of you,
and heaven's kindness lets it pour for hours.

We Are Fine

What we can't do is not that relevant.
We are not able to fly, yet, why should it bother us
that we are not birds, that we are not fish
and that we cannot stay under the surface forever?

Does a tree mind very much who wants to eat its apples?
To each their own. It does not matter to the fish that he
can't sing
nor that he never tasted fruit. Why should we want to know
what we can't be? It is enough, all that we have.

Your eyes can tell me more than I could read in books.
The tree won't know that it needs love,
the fish don't care of lies and truth,
the birds don't see the world in thoughts but only look for
food.

Then you do all of the above. You take me far
though not where I might want to be. You feed my mind.
What we don't have, what we can't do is not what makes us
who we are. That is what I have learnt from you.

You Know . . .

. . . once we made babies
now we make an effort
same difference you claim

Date

It didn't mean a thing this morning:
the dead sparrow with the broken wing
lying on the doorstep in a pool of blood,
the angry faces in the clouds,
the thunder-god, the lightning striking,
that I heard someone sing your song,
it didn't mean a thing to me,
it just came along the day
without it ringing any bell
that I remember.

Autumn can be dark and cold
and death is all around us,
we see a thing in trees that die.
Until I saw the very date,
I got a shock, I screamed and cried,
I realized I was too late,
as we agreed before you went
that yesterday
I should have met you
on the graveyard
a year after the day you died.

Knowledge of Nout

This useless knowledge of nout
randomly invades my eyes and ears
finding a way to be memorized.
During a moment in the shower
when the colour turquoise pops up
out of the blue, I sense a scent
of you here, and other futilities
like moon and candles
laying their light to flatter you more.

It's showing life from sidebars,
I could have done without such fragments
entering my sane reality.
Countless impressions make the ceiling spin
before a squeeze in the sponge
melts all together, mixed colours
in foam, what is important and what not:
all is washed away
by corliosis in the sewer.

Prussic Acid

Your words were berries of the rowan tree,
surprising in greyness of October,
seductive their orange frivolity
when sober thoughts might come and be of death.

The black birds ate the berries anyway,
surviving the deadly prussic acid.
Thus I shouldn't worry what others say,
in placid lines that really mean to hurt.

Like black birds I chewed the fruit, digested,
immune to poison that must come along
with all brightness of the tree, to test it.
I'm strong enough to let your venom pass.

Ending 1

From one place to another, fine.
Goodbyes to make us find some comfort in cold phrases.
Has anyone returned to where he started really?
An astronaut is younger 'cause he has been to space.
The world spins on during our absence
and overgrown the crumbling path will move
while bending slowly for a new direction.
We can't come back.
Our feet are new by every step.
I watch you walk out of the street and you get smaller.
So this new sunlight shines and hurts
as you leave where we once made our start.
Though we don't say the words, both know
this is a silver ending.

Senryu

much was in the way
walls of pain masked the true you
your death made me love
undone of mundane
features in rest emerging
your new pyjamas

Free Gift

What to give you
as the word moon is already taken
by more romantic souls than me,
abused a lot and worn out;
flowers die too soon to linger as a gesture,
while all the feathers of a bird
won't make a bird, and birds
should just be free.
I've entered the bookstore
and realised I don't know the books you like
as much as I thought I did.

Will it mean some,
as I bring you no such presents:
I manage a thought of you in murmuration,
scattered moments such as we have shared,
sound of a thousand wings across the sea,
while no spoken word of mine, no words
can find you, or be heard

in spite of my affection.
Maybe I should give you bread,
something to eat, to emphasize
that nothing is here to last forever.

Should we wait then,
as we both don't know how to move
out of our bird shitted fortresses,
well made from the sand grains that blew over from sea,
solid for unpractical dreams
since all the feathers of a bird
won't make a bird. Still words
won't cost me much, are free.
I have decided you don't need
any more possessions. If you want love,
it's all that I can manage.

Sound

For hours the rain falls.
When we go to bed,
the sound of a million water drops
hitting glass or stone
becomes unheard
in its familiarity
and only when it stops,
we wake up.

I awake when your breathing
is not there, and when the babies
slept in other rooms,

I could hear them silently live
through walls and corridors.
Waiting for their butterfly breathings
made my ears super sonar equipment.

Since then, years went by.
You sigh downstairs in the living room,
I detect coming rain a day ahead,
and I still hear butterflies crying.

Intervals Between Days

Even the worst day ends in night, you say,
they are unimportant intervals,
some healing gaps between the days,
between life and death. A time of unbeing.
So we lie down to peel off the layers
that we needed in the day
and feel our bodies melt together with the room,
becoming one with darkness, absorbed
in silent waiting under roof and unseen sky.

There are some sounds with no existence in the daylight:
all is different now, we go along with
silence but that of the lark that sings,
there is no language which is good,
all is forgotten and forgiven maybe.
My finger finds your chin while I await
your voice returning. I shall not wake you now
because I like the silence of your sleep
as much as the night bird's song.

Making New Herons

The first rains of autumn wash away
the last flowers of summer
and the scent of dead petals
become the fake smell of fall.
We smell up gone roses
as we wander through damp woods
that have no memory
and don't even recall
spring when we found
the young heron,
when all was a promise.
You and I fed it with worms;
still the heron died soon,
we buried it deep but
worms must have eaten it
before the seagulls
took them in turn.
Now we wander apart under
those moist dark trees
while their leaves,
once oily bright green
are crisp and brown
and about to die soon.
The now is not lasting,
we need to think further,
there will be a new spring
with offspring of past,
new herons lay eggs
and new herons emerge

to eat worms and so on
and so on go the seasons.
But herons don't know
and nobody knows
of the reasons.

To Feel That Way Again

I want to feel that way again
like when the rain started to cover
the falling tears of both of us
and our goodbyes still made some sense,
after you were my lover, before we went,
in dark opposite directions, as
never it felt more intense.

I want to be so close again
where leaving each other means the same
as the loss of a torn off limb;
you were a love that sheltered me,
before the rain took your name too far away
to the big stream running below us
into an indifferent sea.

Your Lingering

Among the material that is you
(breathing, body, footsteps)
lingers more, the you that has no name.
I've grown accustomed to its gentle meaning,
sensing you from every distance,
not just by your voice.

Out of the abyss that is time
you will be heard in echos,
in a breeze, in whispers;
I shall remember you
by body, by mind, by affection
as I hear footsteps moving on.

Observed by a Crow

I am the unseen observer,
I saw by accident and held in mind
their togetherness,

their ways of kind and nice,
and later something happened
that I did not realise:

his tired back when he walked away,
her hand that lost all weight and strength
as there was nothing left to say,

she didn't wave him out that day,
he was no lover now nor friend,
the road not having any length

with no beginning and no end:
observed and done, a love is over,
it's all forgotten but by me.

You

Unsaid I knew you were homesick too,
for the flight of geese and autumn light,
for the air that's salt and savoury,
for what lies hidden in our lonely minds, unspoken.
I knew you touched your chin right then
and smiled because of what we share,
unsaid but I am much aware
that you are part of me, and how;
just now I got a photo of yourself
touching your chin, and smiling.

Love on the Mainland

So you took me to your lover's grave
where it rained at the end of summer
and we watched a squirrel
that lived on the graveyard
without disturbing the dead;
we said nothing too.

I saw you dancing with her who died,
both in the sunlight while it rained on,
she gave us her blessing
in the whispering rain
or did you hear her not say
anything either?

The next day as we ate together
the soup which I made that was too salty,
the soup that should warm us,
I cried for the failure,
as it was the dish I cooked
for my first lover.

We drove along a small dead squirrel,
lying on the way to the harbour.
It was all we knew about
the lovers before us;
we shall never know of
those that come after.

Our love on the mainland, strange and wild,
took us back and forth in time and place,
until I stood there on the
cold deck of the ferry;
the last time I saw you,
fading in autumn.
The reed you are.

The reed stands
caught in a flight
halfway to freedom,

stranded in a swamp,
making the best of life.

Waiting in meanwhiles,
like you wait for returning
to the land you have left,
bending waves in all directions,
serf to the ruling wind.

Dreams of what lies beyond
make you whisper at nights

Shelley

It was over between us, and a thunderstorm came.
Books fell down from the shelf for no reason
like domino stones as the grave stones they were,
and my thoughts went with them below,
taking all that was you, they went falling, deep
into the earth taking you. Gone as our love in a blow.

But the wind started turning the pages
of the Shelley I once got from you.
It had to mean something important:
we read it together, lying in grass.
I did not want to look but started reading:
"Alas! This is not what I thought life was."

When It Is Truth

Until we say it out loud: is it true, is it valid?
Or just a thought meandering through mazes of the brain,
making no sense? And let's call it art if it shows up anyway,
through blurred pixels and crummy rhyme. By instrumental
music.
Until thoughts have a voice, no one can argue their rights to
exist.

I have said many words to you that never left my mind.
They went in opposite directions, following moods,
and then rested in dark gates of the cervix.
They are all true although they never saw the light of day.
You just don't know them. And I won't say them out loud.

Nondescript

The nondescriptness of that moment
was what stayed in my memory after we parted,
that nothing had been special enough to have a name:
no clue what colour the furniture was,
what those locals named the food we ate,
how long it was that you and I sat there
on some windy terrace, facing the North Sea.
Nothing happened. Clouds appeared to fade.
But as time went by, pieces fell into place.
I remembered the name of the colour:
mauve. And it came with the memory
of your whisper. The smell of tar,

the lines near your eyes.
My reply. The best moment ever.
Let me describe it like this.

The Stain

After she had removed the stain
caused by her bleeding heart
she decided: never white carpets in future.
She is cleaning the window in rain
and another stain won't go:
the mark where she saw him once more,
the man who would not accept no.

To Find the Truth

To find the truth in you and make it last,
your eyes reflecting what has been unsaid,
a mere reminder of your troubled past,
your shoulders tired of your weary head,
to see the pain in you that hasn't gone,
it all is there in every close embrace.
I feel now time and aging must have won,
your mind is drifting to another place.

On Hold

A layer of frost is hiding you,
cold surface waiting for the sun
and it gets even colder now.
I wait for better moments.
For now everything's on hold,
only patience needed.

Where Now the Poison Ivy
Grows

We walked hand in hand
on a bare shoulder day
when sunlight shone yellow,
caressing gently our skin,
as we touched the fruit
that they sold in the street
and I stole an apple for you.
We walked with bare feet
where the sand gave us warmth
and water washed over
our bodies, our faces.
The salt of the sea
stayed long in our scent
and we ate the ripe fruit
and needed no more
than this and forever.
Your language collided with mine
as the poem you read to me sang

with short rhythm waves like the sea; I
don't know what you told me,
other than summer
was sweet when you and I walked
hand in hand, and bare shouldered,
through that wonderful street
where now the Poison Ivy grows.

Imagine the Night

How to express what I feel for you: I
only have words in a language not mine
but in my dreams you appear in silence.
Nights are better when with you. Even awake.
I feel your shiver going down my spine:
attached, bonded, (please don't call us soul mates).
When I sleep, all seems to be right with us.
My vocabulary sucks but it's fine.
Let's sleep and be together in our dreams.
Imagine the night. Every movement ours.
We stay in bed together till it's nine
and nothing is as it should be, or seams.

Testers

The warm summer air smelled of cinnamon, honeysuckle;
you of travel and sea, tobacco.
Years later they made a fragrance like that,
and sold it in small bottled portions.

They want too much money
for a fading memory, a sense
that is well overdue, but
each time I pass those testers,
in shops between the scents of sweet chemical flowers
—pinkish, or the musky kind—
I spray a bit of long-time-gone in my hair, my neck,
going for free illusions of you. My mind
can't tell the difference;
when I close my eyes, all is true.
If I get a chance, if no one is watching,
more is misting down my skin,
to find you back, retrieving those nights
we secretly claimed as ours.

Holding Hands

We have become
people who don't need
to possess a lot,
for things won't upset us,
nor give us joy,
they are just ornaments,
by standing in life, unaware,
and they can't get through to us;
not like a look, a frown,
not like knowing a love is there,
where no things can reach us.
We have become
almost away from it all.

We have become
people holding hands
on summer evenings.

Sense

Touching deeper than the dead cells of a skin,
stroking more than the dead hair on a head;
we can't seem to accomplish.
What do we know of one another?
Your eyes tell me about lives you lived,
or what has happened since your youth,
but it might be that I just think so.
All we know of each other
is dead skin and hair,
movements that are getting older,
and spoken words, already skeletons of ideas,
making up lies or what we see as truth.
Sometimes we touch without feeling
and some angels never land on a shoulder.
Before I say I love you
I close my eyes and jump into the new
like water holds a heavy loaded ship,
the offspring of the dove won't crash but fly,
it is because the young bird dared to go,
and ships have sailed for ages now, it's proof.
We trust that we won't die. Not knowing how
we try, we dare, because of faith we move.
The new awaits and I go unprepared.

The Flatness of Water

All water lies horizontal by nature;
the field of water is straight,
a mirror of the skies, our solid base.
Water reminds me of you, the smooth surface
not telling of the deep underneath.
The ice you can become.
If I see a wall of water, it means
I am on a capsizing ship (and I was,
but the ship got to port in time).
Water always stays in line,
flat as it possibly can be.
All molecules well-ordered.
Just some of them are surface,
others never make it to the light.
There are no hills of water.
Until a breath of playful air
turns logic overboard,
a twirl, waves, white foam of anger.
Then sea regroups
and flat again
she will continue.

Strand

We built sand castles
and around us children
walls of old fortresses
were tumbling down.

But the sand held on
to dreams and truths
till we let go the grains.
Till we watched sand be smoke.
Around us grown-up lies won over,
dark clouds emerged and
later from the sea
a cold mist came to chase us home.
All was gone now,
but the sun could still be felt
in the palms of our hands.
In the depth of the moment.

Meanings

Meanings changed after what happened,
words seemed the same
but they were no longer exact.
The dictionary needs a dictionary.
The word for love stopped describing it,
and pain, what is pain?
As a Capricorn, I have Scorpio rising.
This means something, so they tell me,
but I am not sure what.
The words are mediocre reflections
of general common notions.
Hidden meanings keep us thinking.
Maybe all poetry should rhyme to satisfy,
there ought to be a standard,
I want so much to reach you. So I try.

Somewhere in the middle, or the start,
or in the end perhaps, of all words is the word *you*.
It is all words. The heart.
What is the meaning of *you*? How
I meant to be a friend, a *you* as well,
but somehow *you* means more now.
You mean more now. Again the truth has bent.
Trust had my latest attention
while, like them all, you went.

Burning Moths

Oh yes I remember that the nights were buzzing.
Cats opened one eye and slept on,
they were old but they waited to die later.
Though the street was a path, the road all gone,
a weeded way to my doorstep was all you needed.

I waited for you and listened while soft rain fell.
Meanwhile waves would bring in shell by shell on the beach.
As buzzing insects died in candle flames,
the cats slept on. Home was us both.
You said you found me by the track of shells.

I hated the sound of rain and silence each,
the covering of crisp small deaths in light
that made me cry, before, unexpectedly at night,
the door went open wide and it was you once more.
No, I didn't cry for you but over moths, I tell you now.

Years later when you lay here beside me
and rain was pouring, loud like always,
buzzing insects cried. You never heard them. You say
moths don't burn in candle flames. The roof went leaking,
some cats died, children came and moved out.

The buzzing went on though, like your stay.
By then we had found reasons, as you told me
why the past was us, that we were like all seasons
and night owls had to die once, anyway.
You seemed to know why life was cruel.

Why did we keep the plates, knives and scissors, the love,
after eating, cutting food, paper, getting offspring—
because we might need all of it again, you said.
Because we cannot do without.
But did we really need the candles?

And you would always look for good alternatives,
trying to find the reincarnations of moths in butterflies,
long after the longing, after the dining, the wine.
The children have their own breed now. Let's save a night owl.
We need not burn the candles anymore.

Out of the Maze

My hand is taking yours,
caressing away thoughts,
the both of us with scars.
My touch can't mend it all

just as your trembling hand
now on my skin, my face,
cannot take all away
of fearful times we lost
whilst running through a maze
of black thorny roses
before we found our way.
I feel your skin on mine
and I see in your eyes
how scars can meet in trust.
We left the maze all right,
we took care of our wounds,
my hand is trembling now.
The roses wilted, dead,
the time we lost is gone
but it has taught us much:
the reason of a touch
and how we should move on.

Intense

The more silent the landscape
the more intense all must be:
a hug in a desert, a war
certainly means more in silence.
No one hears you in traffic noise
and who cares about a battle
with the world dying anyway,
and we're alone now on the beach.
One touch under all these old stars,

why can't this moment be some more
than an encounter of bodies
like so many before us had.
The silence hasn't made us sacred,
our moves are ancient as the world,
but it feels as if we're the first
as no sound but the sea's is here.

Evening on the Island

I see in you what worries me about myself;
reflecting in your eyes my shadows seem to grow
in this evening light, the lighthouse not yet burning
although I have no other way to know the end,
I watch you place the books we read back on the shelf.
We need not knowing what might happen next, right now
the fire is about to start, we need no talk.
I feel your hands touching my face, you show me how
our story has no end. We are one movement, slow,
familiar trust, closing our eyes. We understand.

In Line

We cut sentences in halves and let words float
because we both are afraid to write the truth,
the meanings of the words change so rapidly
from feelings of the gut to abstract drawings.
They are abandoned by reason and get lost.
To stay in line! For ideas it's essential

that the elements of thought don't wonder off,
but this is about us, and it has been so.
We have only said the half of what we want.
(Do you notice I am getting to the point?)
When you don't hear me, being very distant,
I call you by your second name, in whisper,
so only I know that it is you I mean.
I missed a season in which you got a tan.
We seldom meet, only on rare occasions,
with intervals of years, spouses around us,
in the presence of dearest others and wine.
No matter how shattered I know you, or will,
and how little we speak, what you mean to me
stays the same. Still we shall never stay in line.

Joking?

No I don't grasp your wit today, I'm numb;
a cotton cloud is keeping me away,
I live in a tunnel so it seems now.
The hours move without much speed to night.
In here is just a candle flame and me,
a moth is trying to get in, but why?
How can a creature seem to be so dumb?
I listen, I don't know the words you say.
The phone is dead. Outside I hear an owl.
The moth gave up. I dark the candle's light.
Through open windows comes the moist of sea.
I did not grasp your wit today: Goodbye?

Crossing

Cold fish with cold eyes swim through these waters
where green hair is waving under the surface,
fantasy-shaped plankton feeds the species
as we cross the sea by ferry reading books.
We don't know of what goes on beneath us,
our books give us a world to pass our time.
Cold fish with cold eyes swim underneath us.
They live in the bowed ribs of drowned sailors.
Green hair is waving there under the surface,
and we have our coffee, a sandwich, fruit.
Discussing the chapters we read, we smile.
Cold fish with cold eyes swim underneath us.
The repeating engine drum makes us sleep,
while in the ribs of dead sailors fish swim,
the table is trembling, a spoon falling,
some coffee is spilled. We arrive in port.
Where are you going to on the mainland?
I dare not ask you now we are polite.
We had our coffee together, we read.
Once! We knew more of each other. Arriving.
Cold fish with cold eyes stay behind down there,
we don't know of what goes on beneath us,
discussing the books we have read, we smile
as we embark the ship. We know nothing.

A Memory

I was away from love so long
but somehow love caught up with me,
a walk nearby a foaming sea,
a kiss that means we can't go wrong.

For now I'll have to wait and see,
you go away, so much is sure,
who knows what future there will be
and all we know is to endure.

The harbour's filled with ships to leave,
a ship's dog anxious on the deck.
As soon they'll sail, I shall not grieve,
I know one day they'll all be back.

And one of those ships will be yours,
the wind will bring you home once more,
a seagull guiding you the course,
love to be harboured as before.

You Too

I tried to alter how I felt,
make a new plan for coming days,
but every new design proved wrong:
I cannot change the way clouds move,
how seasons flow, the rain that falls,
I am with you in mind and soul.

I went away for a short while
to see the light in different lands,
but everywhere it was the same,
some things can't change by travelling.
I'll travel light in future times,
I only need to bring your name.

And now you told me that you too
are so in love. Now let clouds flow,
let seasons change, whatever falls,
our minds and souls can stand the rain,
we travel only to come home,
and home is always where you are.

Kite

A dream flew like a paper kite
above the clouds of this short night.
It was of you I dreamt, but gone
the kite is. I could not hold on.
Nights are too short to dream all right,
or think of what could be or might,
but if you find my kite by chance,
it means there may be some romance.

The Longest Day

The longest day is when you are not here;
I felt surrounded like a glove by you, and I was safe.
We watched the blackbird make a nest.

You stayed, to drink and pick the berries
that we planned to eat, we were together,
doing well, but not for always.

The air now finds its way over my arms,
my shoulders, before going back to sea.
I shiver as you are not here to glove me.

Since you went, I felt your absence as a draught,
as if your breath is still with me.
The blackbird sings, but you don't hear it.

You left a memory that might do well
on colder days, but it's no shelter
when it rains. When days are grey.

The longest day has started,
the young birds left the nest.
I'm waiting for this day to end.

There is no meaning in the seasons,
not now I wait for you to love me too.
The days should shorten,
cold should come. It doesn't.
Maybe you have forgotten me, like the seasons have.

I didn't eat the fruit,
with my consent the blackbird took it
and this day goes on and on.
I am always waiting for its end.

Breadcrumbs

Sharing bread together as we walk
sometimes I lose you out of sight,
the birds show me where you have been.

I see you limited by what I can,
you watch me and you see the surface,
sometimes our minds meet in a dungeon.

Days go by, we speak but say nothing,
yet, in what is unspoken, I find you.
I now don't need words to read your mind.

Every word we say means: be here with me,
I don't want to lose you over death.
We talk to keep track of each other.

I shall always look for the breadcrumbs
that you leave behind on the road;
their meaning in every conversation.

With Open Eyes

Even with my eyes open the other world invades,
distracting me from what is real. A daydream takes over:
A cornflower field, and red poppies, buttercups,
or an imagined house, with lots of space,
old and mysterious. Kittens, pups, a face. A face.
To sail away I think a sailing ship,
leaving port, losing the cobwebs of the mind.
She goes steady in the wind, the sea is blue,
I wonder what she leaves behind.
And approving smiles show up. A hand on a shoulder.
Sometimes I daydream about you, how it would be,
and all meets up, the best of useless dwellings
is when you sail towards me while I wait
in the meadow near that house,
the best yet to come. With my eyes open to see.

The View

This view is not our lives, but seen from here
we might be part of it. The niceness of
the dancing trees, the clouds, birds going by:
we search each other, trying to be so.

The brick wall keeps us apart from sunshine,
indoors is more darkness, more of the raw
than the roses, the pansies, the rainbow.
The room is filled with books of World War Two.

The TV screen shows horror movies, blood,
words we said keep echoing in silence,
the photos of the loved ones cracked one day,
a dog has died here, some wounds were treated.

But outside a night-bird finds a tune now.
The sun sets with more than expected warmth,
so pink and red, more gracious than we are.
The view is of us. It's what we saw go.

Summer Morning

Pale the day has started out, in watercolours
wearing see-through thoughts that please.
I can see you here, your smile, more so:
your laugh. The fire of the sun just touch and go,
transparency, the kinder side of day.

Then clouds move over and the sky is hard and blue,
a plastic lid that covers what is true,
a tender whisper can't make it here for long,
any subtle gesture wasted on too much of it all,
on the false brightness of summer.

Suddenly all changes again, now rain is falling hard.
Where does this leave us? Give me a clue
before the plot thickens as mist erasing you,
before the paleness of the morning is forgotten,
when all was clear to me and real.

Fixing

Severely into the matter you stand,
bowing for the child with the broken toy.
I like you so much now, and your welcomed help,
your fixing expertise coming to use
as you mend the wheel of the bright red car.

Twirling leaves gather around you both now
to keep this moment fixated in mind.
Maybe one day you can fix some old cracks,
big gaps, loose ends, us both. For now this toy
is my hope that all will once be mended.

Mildly

Days go by mildly now,
your scent has left the building
and the weather might improve at last.
I cannot complain too much.
Days go by mildly now.

We did some universal stuff at times,
remember, like watching a full moon
and making love on a bed with rose petals,
but in my memories
those moments have a kitschy flair.

There was a goodbye in every sentence,
even the items on the table

that were there silently
seemed to scream it out:
Over. Over. Over.
A scissor made me think of pain.

I shall take the kitschy moments
to remember you by mildly,
but not yet. As for a while
I need the pain to understand.
I put the items in a drawer
and clean the table with my tears.

Funeral Oration

Looking into the earth
where the coffin will soon take you down
I try to imprint every grain
as this is where your body will be from now on
for the time it takes to fall back into elements
that need no soul.

But you yourself are not here,
where have you gone to, my friend?
Something of you will stay with me and others
until we in our turn drop dead. A chain.
Parts of what dead people were
remains in dead people to be.

Standing by a grave
never makes me feel better
about nature and the sense of it all.

On the graveyard a woodpecker
machine guns all thoughts down
that could be appropriate.

I suck at funerals, but you knew that.

Cocooned

His face is sleeping now,
his body rests,
he is away in fiction of his mind.

Who knows what he is dreaming.
I count his breaths a minute,
touch his skin, embrace.

White cotton is his warm cocoon
in this early morning air
till he wriggles out of the envelope, I watch.

The giggling sunlight finds his body amusing.
I wonder what goes on
underneath his trembling eyelids.

Where is he now, will he be back?
He turns over slowly,
an arm finds me and then forgets.

His breathing stops, I give a push,
he grasps for air.
I cannot die, because of him.

Because he might be needing me.
Night after night I shall be watching,
not dying, because of this.

Because the sunlight and me are in love
with a man between two cotton sheets.
And he knows nothing of all this. He is asleep.

The Phone Is Dead, Dear.
Thunderstorm.

Smoothly thoughts swift from seagull to crow to raptor.
No moment between awaking and sleep seems to be on its
own,
one thing leading to another: you leave the house in my
good faith
and the phone rings for you, dark clouds appear
while the message cuts the bacon of the day like a butcher's
knife.
Rain starts to fall as the words sink in, bullets hitting the
roof.
There is thunder. A door slam.
The return of the hawk on the nest. Still wet from the rain,
eager to know if someone has rang, you are back.
In one movement, one murmuration, the day has gone by,
and
no. No one has phoned, I say. The birds in the nest close
their eyes.
From hawk to blackbird to lark thoughts smoothly move
backwards,

all fade into dreams, resulting in the good of this morning's
innocence.

Their Moment

But watch her now she thinks she is alone.
The way her shoulders fall so tired,
her hands are trembling as they reach
for the photo frame, she smiles.
Do not disturb her in this moment.
She is with him now in her thoughts,
warm sunlight shines over her white hair,
she shivers as he touches her this way,
their daily ritual before you, nurse,
bring in the hated pills to swallow.
You might catch something of her look
that really was just meant for him
before the shadows fill the room
to start another quiet day. Sedated.

Winner Takes All

When I close my eyes, the chessboard appears,
my thoughts make horse leaps trying to find your king;
my queen stands idle. When I open my eyes,
your kiss means checkmate. Roll over, you king.

Flash. Thunder.

We don't cross each other's path by accident,
we carefully planned it, road map, train tickets,
and then there is you. It has been a while.
We try out small talk.
No, this is not what we thought we would find.
Those years have split us up, changed the chemistry.
There is lightning over the horizon though.
We should take shelter, but we stand
and rain is pouring.
If we are struck now, we die together,
it would mean something, one grand moment.
You put your arm on my shoulder.
It has been great, you say. I say it has not.
Why do you always argue, you say. Flash. Thunder.
When I open my eyes again, you are gone.
I like that ending.

Our Last Murmuration

As you leave there is movement above us,
we stand opposite each other
and watch birds over our heads
flocking like melted together,
turning into new shapes
as if they are one body,
fluently, a quickly changing sculpture in the sky,
round, then longer, then oval,
swiftly flipping from black

to silver to black, a rotating cloud,
made of hundreds of unique individual creatures,
all in one speed, moving like a wave in a football stadium,
and our thoughts can't help but flock in one flow:
they are you and me,
once we were starlings together
dancing, loving, in our mind.
I think I see you smile as you go.
The murmuration is over.

Pass It On

You passed the butter and I touched your hand.
I didn't mean to, but, like electricity, your presence hit me.
My thoughts were: Move on with the bread,
the cheese, please let it happen again.
I never ate so much as then, longing for just the touch
of your skin. Butter might not be good for us, but
the passing of the food was the best thing
that could have happened that evening
when we were both invited for dinner
and we invited the challenge of touch.

Butterfly

It is a moment when I see so clear
our history together in a butterfly,
that comes from nowhere, from a flower,
a precious thing, reflecting in your eyes.

She flies away, my eyes meet yours,
the fire fades as night approaches.
Will the butterfly still live, her one day
almost done. You talk but I don't listen.
I wait for the whispering of wings
in their last moments. Before all this is gone.

Business, His and Hers

You keep yourself disguised in such grey suits:
a tie, a jacket, trousers also grey,
and look like all those men, important. May
your legs find mine, released of my red boots.

The daily dirt is staying in your hair,
you smell of sweat and travelling by train
and on your collar I can see a stain
that won't be gone tomorrow. We don't care.

Your mind is still elsewhere when we make love,
but slowly, by the time the night is gone,
my stroking hands and kisses might have won.
You close your eyes and I know it's enough.

Whenever these fine moments are no more,
it will be on the day that we shall split,
and business won't be like it was before.

Making Love on a Ship That Stands Clear of the Water

Your long legs are pushing mine apart;
like this, near the flood line, I just want to sleep
with you and only water to surround me,
seaweed our blanket,
the sea rocking us to sleep
and clouds drifting over with a smile
till they disappear where the sea drinks them.
Your body sinking into mine,
we make love and the sea is a part.

Art

I see paint on canvas
and register a feel I lost,
words enter the museum
where more people,
maybe all people,
find themselves
gathered for truth
to be revealed,
we shuffle through halls
seeing more than we see
as all was already in us
when we arrived in this building
but now we watch how on canvas
it comes together in paint.

Lover

My hair was a veil and your laughter a dance,
a romance in a weird way maybe.
It was in a library in a place called Paris,
I didn't know anyone there but by chance.
The books all in French must have heard
how my mind was only with you,
when we met in a Baudelaire poem
your hands were becoming a bird.
Your bird then revealed my veil and my cover
in a room with a view of Montmartre.
In your eyes lived a war-struck memory,
twice my age, half my length: my French lover.

If I Could Bid You

If I could bid you firmly with success,
I would bid you firmly not to die now,
nor soon, but to linger a bit longer,
now we found your sock, hurray,
and it is spring, and, look, you did remember
to smile because of the cartoon today.
I have stopped annoying tick-tacks of the clock,
we only hear the nothing of this day,
and in that silence we can make believe
there is no time. No past, no future.
I bid you therefore firmly that you stay,
to be alive some more and be it here so with me.

The Will

All the words you wrote me are now dead
and almost buried in the sand next to the cats,
the dogs, two hamsters, and a parrot.

At the deathbed of your written words I cried
but now and then a bit of life came back to them,
in which I thought they asked me to forgive you.

Now soil is spread above them, they can rot.
I think I'll skip the mourning part for good,
it's best forgotten how you wrote me into love.

I have inherited their images of you,
it was their will that I must always know
your words were true once. And I do.

The Spider Eater

He gave me some flowers that were taken
from a grave he just happened to pass by.
When I asked about it, he didn't say why.
In return, I made him eggs and bacon.

He would eat spiders if that impressed me,
and said one day I'd make someone a good wife.
We were friends in that stage of my life
when spiders were such scary things to me.

He would dance on the stickiest dance floor
if that was what I liked to do, he would,
and ate the rubbish I served and called food,
he asked me afterwards if I had more.

I sometimes see him working on his farm.
He never dances now, he wouldn't harm,
or eat a spider if I asked him to.

One time he saw me and a moment long
I watched him dancing, smiling, heard our song,
and for a moment I was dancing too.

The Last Birds

The last birds have silenced
over waves that are calm now,
on the beach all is quiet
as winter begins.

In stillness, awareness
that all will continue,
I shall believe
in your safe return.

I Need Not Do Life Over Gently

Some hope is built on trembling sand,
sometimes it's just a reaching hand,
some words are lame, like *love* and *friend*,
when rhyme can't cover for my fear
then my work is over here,
I need not do life over gently.
There is no freedom if not everyone is free,
there is no love to lose when you are hating me,
there is no meaning in the word eternity,
when nothing changes for the best,
then let my bones just rot away and rest,
I need not do life over gently.

Paying Attention

You say it in words that matter
but my ears just hear music.
I should listen better
when you say fuck off.

Not Knowing You

After knowing you
there is no more of you
to imagine
in the way I used to
and you used to care.

The Sweetest

Sweeter I can't do
even if I should,
sweeter isn't in my skills.
I can love you very much though,
but sweeter I can't do.

Reductio ad Absurdum

We came together often
though none of us would speak,
we just tore off each other's hair
and sniffed armpits
unintended,
but we understood each other well.

Every postcard after that
lying blue skies
and never I felt more apart
from being together,
but you seemed happy
not touching
not your warm smell
close to my good mornings.

Living under a blue sky
that is lying
on bright postcards,
wish you were here.

The handwriting tells me
in three sentences
you miss me,
but that the weather is good.

You drew a little sun
with a sad smiley.
The rain here almost faded away
the ink of your name.
Proof enough for me.
I love the rain now.

After a Quarrel

When hurt takes over, I can run away
find shelter somewhere else until it's gone.
I have no need to fight the pain and stay,
a coward in your eyes, but then I'm done.
If only words can damage so much good
then should we talk at all about our grief?
The good seems gone from our lives, so would
it not be better seeing one of us just leave?
I need the quiet, walking through the dunes
where thoughts get shape and new perspectives live,
my words find music, blackbirds sing the tunes
and when I'm home again, we do forgive.
We so are human and both had our share,
so no, I won't be going anywhere.

The Rhine

The taste of river air that I took home
exotic as it lingered in my mind,
it gives me back the sense of travelling wild
and images, restored the way they'd been
of summer back when I was seventeen.
I see the weeds on the old river bank,
their colours purple, yellow, white, and blue
and always there the river's silent flow.

While other ships moved faster than we went
I loved the moments on the river spent.
The freedom of the water that I felt
was never greater than when all alone
I hung the laundry out on the rear deck
and waved to other shipmates that we passed
as we approached the German border fast.

The custom officers would enter ship
by stepping in our galley from their boat.
The water of the Rhine could splash on board
and always was the fear of those without
required papers that they'd be found out.

Sweet river air, so heavy warm at night
when on the banks the children that we were
became all grownups during summer nights
and never would a river tell us more
about the loves that there had been before.

Alone Is Not Enough

Standing on two feet, looking with two eyes,
now I know one person is not enough.
Where is the other, and is it really
you, but do you know me then, do I know you?
We open gates and we don't know what's there
until a door squeaks, who are we to know?
Hearing with two ears, walking on two legs
and I know I need to be with someone.
Alone is good for trees, rocks in oceans,
and predators. I need to be with one
to be afraid together over life
and feel a caring bit of company.

Ending 2

it fell like a stone from a cliff into sea and kept falling
the word that you spoke so all was over forever
destroying all what good had been between us
it came as a meteor landing hard on earth
so hard it killed dinosaurs and more
of what we knew to be tenderness
it was the iron castle door
shutting me out forever
leaving me shattered
outside in the cold
it was the word
in that tone
a goodbye
farewell
gone
you
us
I

A Day Forever

If I could give a day a place
inside my mind forever,
this day would be the one
as ships were sailing
on a sea too blue for real
and all was you.
The flowers gave their scent
to the breeze to carry home
and birds sang finer songs than ever,
and all was better than before.

Growing Together

like the sun finds earth
we find us through layers and vales
let's grow together

Slow Days

Going through slow days
I watch the grass grow faster.
The poppies have shadows
moving on, following clouds,
and never return.
All is on the move.
Your absence remains though,
always there, the same wall.
My days become static.
My days are a wall with no shade.
I stand in position and my garden
continues.
How fast does the grass grow
now that you are not here?
How dead
is a wall with no shade?

Tired

I am tired so tired yet sleep won't approach me,
unforgotten are words that now stand between us,
armed with their power they keep me from resting,
forgetting and night, they won't let them pass.
And you don't call and the night can't commence,
I am tired so tired yet sleep won't approach me.

Scandinavian Summer

I found a note the other day
that made me think of piles of hay
and summer, how it was when you
and I were children, going through
some phases in our lives that year.
The hay you lifted in the air
made rain that sparkled everywhere.
We didn't mind our nudity.
You wrote a note you gave to me,
some phrases in our lives that year.
The note proclaims your deepest love,
'twas something we knew nothing of,
we were just children playing games
with what we saw. We had no names,
for days as in our lives that year.

Science

Black is the absence of colour,
yet, if I use all my crayons,
I get the darkest black.
We need a satellite to communicate
though you are sitting beside me.
Is our love on the same wavelength?
If I count all my blessings
I am lacking one on the list.
Or two, three. I wish I couldn't count.

Dying on Your Island

Be not alone in years to come,
as haunting thoughts might kill your nights
and ferries go but won't return.
Be not afraid if life takes off.
A grey day that won't have a night,
you close your eyes and that is all.
But have someone to hold your hand,
if I can't be there, someone else,
and go in quiet blossom rain.

When All Is Over, Is It?

The final stroke to make a painting
makes it a painting. The last words
ever said in life, rounds up a life.
But is the canvas really finished?
Won't conversation go on
somewhere else beyond your time
when you are gone?
Your paint will come to me
in water shades, on trembling days
of summer heat.
You will speak to me through songs
of birds in evening skies.
Do keep some paint, save it for immortal day.
On days when everything is dark
when here on earth your work is done,

when I listen to the blackbirds speak,
I shall think of you and that you are not gone.

Sudden Snow

Sudden snow.
We are warm here,
the fire is burning
spreading orange glow
and we feel a bond
of contemplation.
There is no reason
to make haste, or go.
Outside is now another world
that we don't need to know.
A world we call forgotten.

The Burial

Nothing to look forward to,
all is wasted on me now:
sunbeams can't warm me,
even crying won't relieve me
as my tears have no fluid left,
they are stones.
So much was there
when so much meant you:
the whispering water of the stream
and the sudden rainbow there.

The smell of coffee in the morning
and the jokes you told.
All was you,
my mind was filled
with you.
I connected all beauty
with your presence.
Now I carry heavy pebbles
to where I shall bury your memory,
where it is cold and shady
and no flowers want to grow.

Nightmare

We were on top of the dune,
arms around each other,
watching our united shades
in the warm sand beneath,
when you suddenly let go
and I tumbled
and fell into thorny branches
aching my legs, face, arms;
falling
further away from love,
nothing to hold on to,
all ground disappeared.
Even when I landed,
there was nothing left
but the shade of the dune.

Maybe It Was Passion

A moment ago when your eyes met mine,
just seconds it was, it seemed longer though
it was all in this look; it wasn't fine.
Now I have seen you, your mind I do know.

Of course it is true that all was just show,
maybe it was passion, maybe it was wine?
I should have stayed up, and not looked below
a moment ago, when your eyes met mine.

It was a moment not very divine.
How could our morals have sunk and so low!
We should not have crossed this very thin line,
just seconds it was, it seemed longer though.

We went with the lust, we went with the flow.
About what we did, we should not much whine.
We both wanted love and we did so.
It was all in this look; it wasn't fine.

Had there been time for me just to resign
—and I was in a hurry, apropos—
maybe I would not have called you a swine.
Now I have seen you, your mind I do know.

As we were stuck in this lame status quo,
hoping your motives were not that malign,
I progressed to undress and did it real slow.
How was I to know you strained your spine
moments ago . . .

Organized

My words are neatly organized from thoughts
I gained in time, and follow grammar rules
to have them read and shared with you.
They may not always be the sentences
my mind would like to see,
nor meet your expectations,
but here, this much, is truth
as seen by me, improvement anyway
compared to chaos of a weary soul.
Extractions of my inner world.
So bear with me and know
I try to write how much I love you
but in a different verse each time,
where nothing rhymes, in longing for
your understanding of the whole.

In Lakes the Ground Not Seen

In lakes, the ground unseen,
my thoughts of you must find a grave,
the depth of water I don't know.
They ought to go and give me rest.
They might swim east,
fine swimmers as they are,
or float more west,
or sink into the mud deep down.
I do not care. I need them gone.
I'll tie them with a brick for weight,

as they should not emerge too soon.
My thoughts of you must find a grave
in lakes, the ground unseen.

I Compare You to a Bat

If a bat decides not to hang upside down,
is that a defected bat,
or does that mean
a new species is born?
You don't fit in, so it seems,
but maybe the world doesn't fit into you.
You are a bat,
and you won't hang upside down.
Maybe you are the first of many
with a new way of thinking
and will you fly out of the cave,
not in darkness, but when the sun shines.

Renewing Vows

Renewed is life now it is spring,
what was in earth, in womb, in tree,
unseen and small, is peeping out,
is given birth, is blossoming.

I see the flowers almost here,
my fingers pick the first of them,
I smell the new born lamb, the blood
that lingers on its mother's rear.

Now sunshine warms up the cold ground,
the land is waiting for new life
and sounds of birds are everywhere
as they are mating all day round.

Be here with me in this new way,
we start again where we went wrong,
be close to me now, make us one;
apart we wouldn't bloom a day.

A Goodbye to Some Thoughts

Some thoughts I leave behind in sea
no longer more a part of me.
They can drift off to other strands,
it's here where our acquaintance ends
and if they shipwreck somewhere far
I hope it will be where you are.
Please bury them with some respect;
they once were thoughts, of you, in fact.

Spring Nights

Dark blue is staying for a little while
as grey has passed away in the last hour.
The light feels better now, it's almost night
and geese are flying over our isle.
In nights like this there is no misery
but only gratefulness for being here.

My love is sleeping in my arms till dawn,
what he might dream, will stay a mystery.
And in the morning other birds will sing.
They flew from far to stay till winter comes.
The morning light is waking up my love,
the room is golden now, the shade of spring.

Hear the Wind Howling

hear the wind
when howling
I always heard
your cry then
be
with me
in remembrance
if not in thought
when
it gets darker
now all is over
hope has no symbols
to matter or care
no more
be with me
here is our place
on the shore where
I wrote my last letter
hear the wind
when howling
and maybe hear
my cry then

Rendezvous

let's meet here
where the wind is ruler
rearranges landscape
that is shaped by
moving oceans
and high tide
tired waves die calmly on the shore
prior to return in deeper water
nothing seems to last
all does move
sand is blown to form new dunes
while howling sounds surrounding us
never change their tunes
let's meet here
when all is almost over
and there is no more
going where the waves die calmly
prior to return in deeper water
meet me halfway on the shore

The Elephant

We lived with an elephant in the room,
pink and with the size of Texas, it stepped
on toes, putting chips on our shoulders.
It lived with us for years, then we killed it
with sarcasm, and buried it outside.

All participated in the murder,
but the elephant was never mentioned.
We started to feel guilty of the crime
and the space we gained, soon became choking.
Another elephant now lives with us.

X-rays

I'm amidst a birthday conversation,with six people talking
at the same time,
words leapfrog through the living filled with smoke,
exploding in laughter. I lost track somewhere
between the price of fuel and the weather.

Then, out of the blue and cigaret fumes
you enter. So we are back together,
miles apart. Your eyes hardly remember.
Photos are taken, the flashlight x-rays
prove I'm with strangers now. I should have known.

Lasting Truth

To find the truth in you and make it last,
your eyes reflecting what has been unsaid,
a mere reminder of your troubled past,
your shoulders tired of your weary head,
to see the pain in you that hasn't gone
it all is there in every close embrace.

I feel now time and aging must have won,
your mind is drifting to another place.
Then, like a flower on a winter's day
it is your smile that makes the sadness fade,
and joy is felt, your past drifted away,
new truth is now another memory made.

Till Then

I watch you watch the clouds go by
and geese going the same speed
I see the longing in your eye.
Will they come back, and will we meet?

Storm

I watch the sad clouds move over the sea
while sand is blowing you out of my mind.
I'll worry no longer of what has been
but go with the gulls that fly in the storm,
onwards, away and forever myself
and the golden sun is returning now.

Trying to forget I am lost here now,
I'm standing near the black turbulent sea
thinking how much there still is in myself
that I don't know, discovering my mind.
On and on waves are rolling in this storm.
I walk on, to where I have never been.

We could have had love, and we could have been
together, watching these gulls leaving now,
see them flying bravely towards the storm.
We'd sit on a dune thinking of the sea.
Not a worry, not a care on my mind
and I could have had you all to myself.

But I am not here now to think of myself.
Pondering over all that might have been,
I decided you are gone from my mind,
so why should I keep wanting you here now
as if it would be: you, me, and the sea
both sheltering in your coat from the storm.

To blow away these thoughts I searched the storm
but I can't always keep fooling myself,
this is what was whispered over the sea:
It was in vain, I never should have been
here, thinking I was over you by now,
as the truth is you haven't left my mind.

Just as I am starting to doubt my mind,
a man, you, walks towards me in this storm
and you spread both your arms to hug me now.
You know me better than I know myself
and knew this was the place I would have been.
Your coat around us both, we watch the sea.

Light

Thinking of the light that sneaks in just in time
from a hidden source to save the greyish day,
like candles lit in darkened rooms
where mothers wait in vain
and stars at night in cloudless skies
guiding whom are lost,
or as a ray of sunshine
entering in a sudden, unexpected way
would lift you up with cheer,
lighten up your heart
to last you through the next, new year;
thinking of you,
I wish you that, and more.

New Colour

The haunting images you knew about, are fading
into pale aquarelles softly whispering of the past,
and we go on
as I learn of your reasons of sadness too.
We can only find ongoing life in this madness
in not being scared of the rest
of the world.
The images, drawn in haste
with harsh coal, now give colours
in a world that is whole.

To Feel That Way Again

I want to feel that way again
like when the rain started to cover
the falling tears of both of us
and our goodbyes still made some sense,
after you were my lover, before we went,
in dark opposite directions, as
never it felt more intense.
I want to be so close again
where leaving each other means the same
as the loss of a torn off limb;
you were a love that sheltered me,
before the rain took your name too far away
to the big stream running below us
into an indifferent sea.

II

The Road to Myself

Journey to Yourself

When you go to other places, leaving
home behind, forget what you expect to
find, for greater must the finding get you.
Light that, either gold or silver shining,
dances on the sea, the sky is turquoise,
grey, it might be damping, misty, raining.

Don't imagine sunshine, how it falls there.
Meet those moments—blank and mindless, humble,
eager, hungry—stepping down, away from
you, the self, and watch him, nosy, walk through
unexpected lanes and roads, before the
journey home, returning to the city.

Our Shared Fate

We share our fate in languages half learnt,
our words have traveled days of evolution,
in nights our dreams make how we think
and make up for illusion.
We say more than we know.

Combine the two, the day and night,
and we can speak of destination.
Maybe our fate is that we cannot stay for long,
we carry so much burden on our road,
we cope and think that heavy lifting makes us strong.

We die although we always thought we would not.
But now and then we may return in quotes,
in déjà vus and photos,
in names and hastily written notes.
We could not disappear, or so we hope.

Apart We Stand

Apart we stand as thrown away from love,
alone and tired, waiting for a ring
but no, the phone is dead and I won't sleep
as well as when your breathing follows mine.

Apart we live our lives through thick and thin,
for what it's worth, I never loved again,
I miss your presence, your reclining chair.
No I don't care that you don't ring at all.

We lie our lives pretending all is well
but nothing is, we stand as thrown away,
apart we are alone, and tired we move on.
I shall not phone you but I miss your voice.

The Deal

Look here, life, I said, you can take it or leave it.
I am not going to change, not anymore so,
for this is my body and this is your home now.

Every breath I take is well intended fresh air.
So let's be friends. I shall accept all of your flaws
until the last day that we might spend together.

Care for us both if I forget to nourish you.
Kindly remind me that we now are friends not foes
so we can go on, I said, in some harmony.

Go Not

Go not without a memory of slumber,
remember the turquoise and the gold,
the brightness of the room in summer.
Go not without, before you go away.

If I have failed and nothing makes you stay:
go not without hearing the growling sea
before you go, the waves that rolled forever.
Go not, go not without a memory of me.

Cloudreading With a Goose

Clouds tell me of places,
shapes emerging and fading—
none might ever appear again.

I'm the only one here
to see these figures explode
when a wild goose is joining me.

As we're watching the sky,
we understand each other
and I become the wild goose now.

Tranquility

a spring butterfly making silent leaps
as it jumps to the sky and returns,
the sound that you hear when there is no sound,
the blue that you see when there's nothing to see:
tranquility

Mischievous

Mischievous you were in your enticing elegance,
I liked our ligaments, our naughty, numerous
and humorous adventures with no dirty dissonance.
This was no decadence, as you seemed gentle, generous.

At times you acted so fantastic and amorous
but there is nothing glamorous in being bombastic.
I am not sarcastic, just trying temperance
because my tolerance is not forever elastic.

Though your attention has been pouring plentiful,
so beautiful, giving my life a dearest dimension,
I dread that your pretension is very villainous.

You were too lecherous in this clever contention,
in my retention I have too many memories
of miseries, and you were mighty mischievous.

Evergreen

Evergreen are meadows in my memory,
their mold and draught are far, forgotten
though my head owes room to this sweet scenery,
my sons, now old, but both begotten
out of love, appearing in illusion,
a dearing illustration how I roughly remember
the raw contradiction in days of cruel confusion,
the cold of snow that covered in darkest December
what dared to try and fuel life under solid surfaces
with plants living as wildest wintergreen
the silent time so used for pronounced purposes;
memories are giving enigmatic evergreen.

Museum of the Mind

As child I stared at canvas, stone and wood
where nothing was revealed, no sound to hear,
the quiet in the room, the solemn mood:
museums seemed a place of mold and fear.

The cracking of the old gallery floors,
although the rooms were empty but of me,
the brutal slamming of unopened doors
and paintings that showed more than I could see.

Perhaps I was too young to grasp the art
but beautiful those memories still feel
of antique buildings, silent days alone.

I keep the memoirs housing in my heart
where no decision stands of what is real
as every art is truth within its own.

Seconds of Eternity

It was there, but gone the other moment:
a thought, solution for a problem,
then—no more,
one of those clouds the wind blows out of shape,
dissolving in cerulean sky, or
a key, one of a kind, melted back to steel,
returning to the cluttered chaos of the mind.

I have found that unseen "there" at times:
between the deformed fragments of my past—
a lump of underheld emotions,
a deep dark pit
of possibilities and spite, with
every now and then a bright idea
that will never make it to the surface.

After the Night Before

In early hours will the daily din
awake you out of dreams with fractioned view,
this moment all the world seems strange and new
to make you feel a nosy alien.

The day is waiting for you to begin,
the windows covered yet in morning dew,
outside some vague contours, a lonely few
already drunk, same state as you are in.

Some coffee might just do the trick you know,
make you forget the reason and the cause,
for drinking through the night as you have done.

Ambition, money, job means you must go.
Another grey spot in this world with flaws,
you feel revived, your hangover is gone.

Identity

I'm not my pain,
it is an alien
trying to take over,
not what should remain.

I'm not my fears,
they are vicious shadows
living in my nightmares;
I am not my tears.

My identity by choice
would be a writer,
woman, friend, and lover,
free, using my voice.

Free

My home is sand and water and your thought,
to dwell in them is how I feel at home,
from shoreline towards dune I walk and roam.

A prisoner maybe I am, and caught
by promises of love and making home
though free I feel, like sea waves topped with foam.

You could not keep me here if this was not
what I had wished for, what it was I sought,
I would not stay and live on silty loam
if this was not the place that I call home.

Cynosure

Polaris, you matter now
after what has been
attracted to your brightness,
guidance on my journey.

Looking north for you
during the sunny day
your presence giving strength
my eyes find light.

Attractive is your brightness
known by all sailors
even when it's day
you guide me, Polaris.

Slowly Walking

I'm slowly walking,
sensing wilderness,
each step outdoors
discovery,
each walk a new adventure.

Watching time,
measured in clouds
and hearing grass grow,
overcrowds,
abundancy lies underneath my feet.

Slowly I shall walk back home
to the self I left behind,
to the talk
and to my mind that took all in.

Unwritten Chapters

I wonder what you think
when we lie in the grass,
your head resting in my lap
as if you are a book to read
and you sleep, or pretending.

What are your thoughts about,
of what do you dream? I don't know
what to think of the cover
until you open your eyes;
then your mind is an open book.

I read how your story went
from childhood until now,
to where the empty pages start.
After that, each chapter
should be a romance in spring.

The Smallest Thought

Seen through empty bottles
much brighter looks future:
green light no shadows
but headaches will come.

With this bed I thee ring
in worse and for the better
to belove and hold on to
till one is leaving in awe.

There are lace memories
beds covered with petals
wooden floor and bottles.
Enough said. You're gone.

Tension

The world can best be kept out,
no one entering the house, phones out,
no television, only sounds
of nesting blackbirds
for whom it's just another spring.

If That Time Comes

What would you grab if we
had to leave the house in a hurry?
I know you—probably the toothpaste
or a tin opener, your Swiss knife
instead of photo albums, things I gave you,
or framed pictures. Our letters.
What of me would you take with you
if we were to be separated by force?

Maybe you would make time to search but I doubt
that anything of me is to accompany you,
dragged through fire, water, gunfights,
while I probably shall find myself
carrying a trunk full of

almost forgotten moments of us
and all the way to whatever safety
not for a second letting it out of my sight.

After You

I won't recover easily from you,
back into the earth of loneliness I'll go
with the smell of decay,
alone, remembering, all bones
and skin and useless will my body be
but it once knew how to please you.

So will my mornings be,
every morning and every afternoon
I shall be dying more away from you.
Away from you, an unbearable phrase
as is the thought. The truth in words
that I cannot say without fear.

My afternoons will be filled
with reading your letters out loud
and hearing words from when we had no idea,
from before our hands held each other,
before our eyes met,
or was it after? The ink is fading.

So will my evenings be,
in twilight when your shadow seems to haunt,
when silence kills my screaming

before the night takes all of me
in dreams. Of course I shall get over you,
I just won't recover easily.

Strength

When the deep
is under your feet,
you are falling,
black walls closing in
and all seems over.

No one can help you there
but it is not over.
This fall with no length will end,
reality coming back in time,
your loneliness a phase.

You will find the stairs upwards,
the hand reaching out to lift you out of the deep
is already there for you.
It is your own hand.
It is your own strength.

Life Probably Is Not

I know what it's not to me: Life.
It is not about experience
although one could look back in time

and be content: "so much achieved,"
one could be mute and angry too,
whatever: I shall make some notes.

Life is not the voyage to death;
that is only the dark side track,
that we die—not that important.
What makes life our reason to be?
Maybe I know what life is not.
However, I make notes and see.

For me so far life was a dream,
a journey, an adventure too,
a waiting to be found and find.
Discovery. To learn and give,
a life to live is worth it all:
all pain, each downside, and the fall.

Train Thinkings

The train is starting to leave the platform.
I look outside, the landscape tells me it is colder now.
Across me sits a woman in no mood to talk,
a man is reading in a paper.
On the front page a picture of a woman with a veil.
Even she is shutting me out.
And so I wander off in thought.

What does this all mean? Have I shut out myself as well?
To let in myself from outside me what will I find in the corners

of my mind once I have dropped my veils for myself?
With my luck, probably a king size mirror.
The thought makes me smile out loud.

The man puts down the paper, the woman starts to talk.
I now see that they are together.
"It is getting colder," I say, as their eyes have made me their
accomplice. And within a minute, we are discussing climate
and the Sixties, when winters were real. But last year was
severe as well. Yes it was.

The paper, now redundant, lies open, a picture showing a
smiling face.
A winking eye.
They reach their destination.
The paper and I have a long way still to go.

Eyes Meeting in a Train

The train shows how we changed the world since then
but do you care much, hidden in your book?
You travel best without having to look
at landscapes being filled with filth of men.
I notice that you lick your lips at times
and watch you smile because of prose you read.
Then there's a second, where our eyes do meet.
You speak. "I don't like poetry that rhymes,"
you say. "Do you?" And I search in my mind
to find an answer that is true yet kind
as you have eyes that make me love this train.

"I do at times," I say, then you read on.
The splendour of the moment now is gone,
the world has changed some more and we have rain.

Accepting Some Delay

The train is going slower
due to another train in front of us.
At five p.m., it is already getting darker.
In the window I see myself, but older now.
So much to think about
of how lucky, glad I feel,
and why it is that I am happy;
a word no poet ever seems to use.
Counting my blessings,
not leaving you out by the way,
I watch the grey turn into black.
Still so glad I live, a feeling
too mundane for?
I've known times that were not really mine,
when I couldn't live my own life.
All it took to change, was stepping out
of stupid situations, getting nowhere.
The train is speeding up
and my thoughts are slowing down
into the deeper meaning
of acceptance.

Leaving

the train a zipper
opening the white landscape
snow covers the track

I won't come back
I won't come back
I won't come back

silence left behind
sheep didn't even notice
I passed them so fast

The Maze

Lost at times in time and mind and never really found,
playing hide and seek with shadows of your past.
Emotions are best players in this game.

Lost, your name is mentioned nowhere, no familiar voices,
you have no one to go to, thoughts live in a maze.
To be alone is not a phase; it is forever.

Lost again and this time serious, an end,
here is no difference between your nightmares and reality.
Now all is lost and life is over: this—you know.

Found as you are in what is called psychosis
and this means constant nightmare. No escape.

A prison cell where you hear screaming in the darkness.
But you won't tell. No, you won't tell. You promised.

Demented in My Dream

In my dream already I'm demented,
I don't remember how to catch the ferry.
Like on a square, how to know where you are
when all the houses seem to be the same.
To buy a ticket, I am running up and down, get lost.
I'll be too late, I call, people are watching,
eyes with unhidden scorn.
There are trains too that I shall never catch.
In my dream I still am myself,
but more and more forlorn.

Finding Lost

Some fragrance takes you back
while you are not prepared,
a thought gets lost among distractions,
and what it was that you were searching,
you forgot.

Your steps return. The task undone,
although you feel as if you gained
new energy that's coming with the flow.
You can go on and each time you get lost again,
it will be so.

The Forgotten Poem

Sad poems brought me into tears
and funny ones seemed shallow,
I didn't find what I was looking for in text,
I needed for my mind to be above it all,
allow it to fly out, away from daily life and pain.
I had no clue what I was searching.
It took me years, the poems gathered dust.
And then a window burst and opened,
a breeze walked through the books
in a sudden sunlight beam,
to show me where to find the page.
I read this poem in new light,
it took me over oceans full of drowning cries,
it was the heartbeat of the storm I heard,
I saw new colours and swift murmurations
of blackbirds dancing in each word.
The poem entered me, became my blood,
and every line went on
to deepest corners of my soul,
it took me over, thus became a new nail to my coffin,
I understood now what life was about, 'twas then
the window shut, the light was gone,
and I fell back to earth,
the book all torn, the page now gone.
I never found the poem back.
I wish that I remembered.

Alone

To stand alone again in morning light,
after another argument of wasted words,
yes, you know to hit them where it hurts
but you don't realise you do so at the time.

One day you'll know what they expect from you
and more so, what is better left unsaid,
but for the moment, alone again you stand, and tread
into the morning light that is too eager pleasing.

To Be There

I would like to be in a place for a while
where only hasty people live,
where streets are treeless gutters
and noise is all around me,
the smell of human nature in colognes
streaming out of bank offices
and everywhere plastic, lots of bright coloured plastic,
I would like to be there
just to be homesick.

My Leave

I am taking the day off being me,
today I am what you are looking for
and I shall behave accordingly:
cook that food you like and that kills you,
laugh at your jokes but not too loud in public,
and I won't say snappy things nor give my opinion
and I won't mind that you hardly listen nor read what I write
as I know you are so much more important than me
and of course you can do anything as you please—
I am not me, so go right ahead.
Yes that odd position how you always wanted to take me
and no I don't mind if you snore all night,
scream in your sleep and kick.
But do remember by dawn
I shall be back from my leave,
refreshed. New.
A better person.

October Sunrise

Forgotten that I hadn't come to find,
I found without searching what I got right here
and all of it in one October sunrise on the pier.
My mind just needed to remember.

Angst

What died inside of me and comes alive in darkness
I fear the most as through its eyes
I saw the curtains be tormented faces,
the child died in my arms
when it did not that time, the cutting knife.

It's memories of waiting in a place of mud,
a blanket all around me and a mother figure,
but I have never been there,
still I feel and smell the nearness of our death,
more real than I could have imagined.

Although I think that chemicals have killed the demon,
the therapist who yawned a lot
extorted it with reason, I know it's there.
Its offspring waits.
It cannot be aborted. It got eternal life.

Autumn 2

The cold and silenced grey of autumn never liked me,
it throws bitter glimpses at me from behind the dying trees.
All over autumn's face mortality is written,
my make-believe of going on forever and forever young
stumbles crippled in the wood to hide in a deserted hole.
A mist outcasts me from all colours, I feel locked in
and hated throughout winter. This is no illusion but the truth
and will be so until the light of April comes my way.

To Leap an Abyss

An abyss on either side of me
I stand and wait for senses to return.
It's dark and every step I take
means falling back. The crumbling road
behind me is already overgrown with
strings of ivy that won't let me go,
and purple toads are watching in the shades.
I have no choice. I take the leap
and I shall do so every day
until I am where I can rest. Where I am me.

Reunion

The person, sitting quietly opposite me
at the wobbly round table
that had carved names in the wood
of those we both remembered well,
had aged more than I could imagine.
After neglecting our friendship,
not much was left of whom I'd searched before.

Where went youth, the smile, the energy?
Still some familiarity was lingering
in eyes and lines, and features one by one
came back to being those that I once knew.
The person had been lost for years in dust,
in fading mist and pretences, in cold denial
and darkest corners, waiting for forgiveness.

There had been no kindness, love,
just hate, regret and shame, but now,
in this September sunlight, see,
a bit of understanding came between us.
We found each other and it was enough.
I recognized the person well
as I could hide no longer from myself. As it was me.

My Cane

My cane has a history
as it was bought by my mother
many years ago for my father
one day on the mainland
when he could not walk anymore,
later also used by her,
and recently by my son when he hurt his knee,
and now this stick is my companion,
my way to stay mobile;
best friend and ugly as hell,
our relationship started on the wrong foot anyway
as I tripped over
but now I am used to its ways
and know how walking should be done.
My cane is now on what I do lean,
my cane and I go steady, so:
come on world. We are so ready!

The Treasure

The sand was blowing over land,
my eyes not ready for this rage
saw nothing but a mist, as then
a man appeared, not sure his age,
his pace was tired, old and slow.
Near the swash mark he was searching,
the tide was low and water gone.

I approached him while I wondered
what had brought him here in storm.
He looked at me and said my father's name
before he went away and just walked on.
They had been friends and when
he let some nice wood go to drift away,
I knew the reason why he came:

He had to find himself again.

I Shall but Not Now

There still is more to learn
from you, from nature, to explore,
there still is time to turn a leaf,
to make a point, to see, achieve;
a chance of ever to be wise.

So why can I not seem to rise,
and start the day the way I should?
I'm in my bed, and all is good
and well. Around me life is moving on.
I shall take part. I shall I shall.

Sad Days on the Calendar

There are days
I can be sad for seasons,
many reasons to be down
but they are days
just as the good ones,
each a treasure, each a gift;

maybe pleasure is no measure
and this life has many ways
to find meaning, if we sift
the sorrow out of graveyard sand.
If we can see the bigger picture.
If we reach out to someone's hand.

In the meanwhile I am trying,
coping, hoping, effort making
though my body is forsaking,
friends are fading, light is grey.
Every morning is a challenge
when such sad days seem to conquer.

Then to notice someone's caring,
then to see a smile, kind eyes
and I know this all shall pass
if I hold on to the last straw
of my sanity, myself.
Sad days lose their rights in time.

Guilt

The air moves from your gesture to the tree
to move a leaf and make it fly away
across the street to land in someone's tea
before it's swallowed and the person dies.

You find a shell that washed ashore one day,
giving memories of when you were child;
this one, no other shell around could say
the stories of those times you almost drowned.

A whisper tells you where to go from here,
tall trees move gently as you walk beneath,
they say the neighbour should be drinking beer
instead of tea. It's not your fault. It's life.

Black Roads to the Mind

On the black tarmac road
next to the silent driver
in the rhythm of the engine

thoughts emerge to live a little,
growing into adulthood as poems:
oversized obesed sestinas,
frolicking free verses
or remaining youngsters, the size of a mere haiku,
before they die in the gloom of red traffic lights,
and buried quietly next to the dead sheep on the moors.
Then we go on and the driver never looks back.

Words That Linger

The words that linger in my mind, are those
I should have long forgotten, but I chose
to keep them living where they hurt me most,
reminders of the cruelties. I host,
until I find it possible to part
with all distress that makes a bleeding heart,
the words that told me I was not worth love.

Persona

What am I but my thoughts: a short mortality
to be eaten by some worms
after life that I passed on.
But thoughts are not my thoughts alone,
the words they use, I haven't stopped creating.
So then, what is my part in this,
to rearrange what's not my own?
Archaic fears in lines that have been waiting

somewhere inside myself, is that then what it is,
what should have been?
In every mirror, a different me looks back
to what remains unseen.

A Book to Never Finish

Every line in this story has a meaning to spot,
makes a new horizon in what it might say,
each skyline under a new leading,
each phrase gives more away
bringing questions, that
are heading for the plot.
I want to know the end of the story
but I don't want to finish the book.
Yet.

Finding My Way

Finding my way back
to self-respect and the water tap,
I try not to stumble
over empty bottles and skeletons
that fell out of the cupboard.
How fine is the taste of water.

September

September now, a summer gone,
I am not ready for this change.
The days already feel so old,
the leaves no longer fresh and crisp.
My winter clothes still out of reach,
I hate those knitted sweaters each
and every one: reminders of
the dark cold days approaching soon.
The sun was such a real good friend,
of course our time now has to end,
this is the way the seasons are,
a moment with a sunshine smile.
This friendship lasted just a while,
yet, I'm not ready to let go,
not looking forward to the snow,
I loved this summer, what it meant:
The light, the warmth; it will be far
away from us for months to come,
so I shall try to dream me some,
to tide me over for the winter.

Peace

A lot goes on elsewhere but here is silence;
no harassment will take place when I'm alone
and rain can fall without disturbing peace.
I could pretend no other lives in the whole universe.

Somewhere you are around me though.
It seems that distance doesn't matter now.

A lot goes on that I am not aware of,
so often I don't understand the why and how.
One day this Earth is dead. We humans kill
whatever we can kill, we are that breed
and always will be so. In Syria they know.

But here I can pretend the world is good.
I watched the full moon shine over the water.
So quiet can it be. Deceivingly at ease.
There is no peace but when I am alone
why not pretend for just a moment that there is.

Outnumbered

Lying in bed on my side
I push the world back for a little longer.
Thoughts flutter and return to silence.
I want no part of what is turning around
beneath my head. Beyond my sleep.
I'm slumbered.
But with the curtain moving,
sun spreading yellow on the wall,
the smell of coffee, thoughts of you
that slip in secretly by songs of birds,
I roll over and give in to another day.
Outnumbered.

Reader's Block

Maybe it's me. I am getting more stupid
and I can't understand what I read, nor feel
the hidden meanings of poems, but it could
also be that the poems are the problem.
I try to see an image as shown in lines
but I don't know what the words mean or should say.
I try to follow an original thought
but get lost in weird constructions that bother.
What others tell me, I suddenly don't hear,
my daily read is not even disturbing.
This must be reader's block then. Does that happen?
I am not into Neruda and Shapcott.
My mind needs to unwind from the poetic
and only take in light, not absorb the dark.
Maybe it's me. I am getting more stupid
and can't understand the words nor the real me.

Summer Night

We are numb by the lasting heat wave,
our bodies wait for the night to pass
and nothing lasts in our memory.
Words we said once, now keep a distance
and stay hidden in wallpaper shades.

Here we had children, in this old bed
they came from you and me together
from another world, another time

here they started. Here we shall end too.
The curtains dance on the thunder drum.

Why do I think of life and death now,
as lightning seems to want this moment
kept for eternity, you and me
and the furniture that knows it all.
Our naked bodies have no secrets.

The sheets are cold in this time machine,
our bed, a cover for a moment
as the cool won't come this night. Won't stay.
Numb we move away from each other,
waiting for the outburst of cold rain.

What to Take With Me

I shall not take much to the grave when
and I shall not think too much about,
a hopeless battle is the one where
immortality can't win. I shall not take much
but I hope to leave a lot behind.
A footstep in the sand just stays a second
and I shall not think too much about
what I've accomplished is so little. I shall
just take with what I came. No more.
But I hope to leave a lot behind.

The Art of Sitting

There is no hope for me,
I'd rather sit and think of nothing much
than go outside to watch a full moon hang over a cobalt sea,
than go to places where to find a mate and romance of the
flesh,
than find a cause more noble or more fun.
I need no fun, I sit.
The music can't lure me away from my feeling of
contentment.
The cool of silent evenings gives me more than my need of
applause.
There is no hope that I shall live the fullest life, for I am me.
The empty spaces in my thoughts are there to fill the
thoughtless gaps.
Though much resentment comes from others as I sit,
I have to sit.
This is it. To sit and think of nothing much.
Just of life perhaps.

Alchemy

I try to kill the pain with something chemical
that I cannot pronounce nor swallow well.
I only know if I take all the pills at once, I'm dead.
Someone has mixed some kinds of poison
to make a medicine, or at least he calls it so; imagine
the hunchbacked alchemist in his mouldy dungeon.

The toad he must have tried it on went all purple just before
it died.
The crazy alchemist is laughing.
Among the seven other pills I take is now his magic
blending in,
from my stomach to my guts.
All is entering my blood.
A dead toad's resting on the slimy stony stairs,
the alchemist makes potions now of a lizard's eye. It's night.
Meanwhile the pain's not going anywhere, like any hero it
will not die but fight.

A Personal Note

I shall not be so arrogant to say life treats me wrongly,
such whining!
Life is as is, and pain is part of life. We all suffer
one way or another. But I do dream, of love, of friends,
of how I should dance over meadows.
How I would live, if possible.
A mountain doesn't feel such pain or joy. Perhaps
an avalanche won't bother him. A mountain's view is boring.
I am no mountain. I am, you are;
the mountain is not, but a rock.
I can go, I have a choice to change, to feel, to give.
Life is a gift and I give too. Maybe it was too little.
Now I can wait for what comes next,
or maybe do some more exploring. Like a mountain
I can wait forever though, to find kindness in a voice.
What makes me go is friendship more so over passion,

a perfect body is a body now that lives. I changed my values
and I noticed so have you. Life treats us well.
It is the mountain who should be complaining.

Small Proof

I don't want so much from life
now that I know a little of the taste of fruits,
somewhat of the love that's friendship,
much of my own imperfection,
and most about what life has not in store for me.

I ask for small proof that I matter,
yet even little things are not for me,
I don't know why. The fruit tastes bitter.

Underneath

Underneath the luggage
that you carry with you
in overheated diesel trains,
on buses, boats, and taxis
is your ticket home,
cracked and torn, but valid.

Looking for Rainbows

I should have stayed in bed today and made the rainbows up.
Instead I went to look for them but none appeared at all.
Now coffee is awaiting me, as faithful canines do.
I should have had my coffee first, so I had realized
that rainbows only show when rain has fallen too.

Future Plans

One day I shall live the way I want:
wearing sweaters that belonged to lovers
on a ship that won't sail anymore,
writing, and there will be cats and flowers.

Poppies will grow in pots on the deck
and every word I write will be mine,
one day we shall hoist a piano on board;
whoever likes can play. One day.

The Search

The need of finding
stuff that got lost,
ideas that yet have to be,
new colours, scents, sounds, sentiments.
Foods. The search is more intense,
meaningful, worthy, immense

than the find. The result.
Or is it that I looked for lesser goods?

Braveness

I avoid daily problems
like, when trying to cross a road
with too much traffic,
taking a walking detour seems to make it easier.
But the daredevils zigzag
between cars and bicycles,
risking their lives to be there first
and they think nothing of it.
Maybe the best way to deal with problems
is to run into them with your eyes closed,
pretending immortality exists
as perhaps that is braveness.
Maybe the best way
to deal with braveness and daredevils
is avoiding daily problems
and staying safe.

Inside the Mess

It shows I've lived;
I got my stitches,
my scars, my scares,
my soul's been trashed
and I survived

the rape, the drowning,
the craziness,
but I'm still here
and stronger too
because I found
the me inside the mess.
Strong. I never thought
it was applicable to me,
the frightened child,
the dominated wife,
the promiscuous lover,
the boozer. The person
outside the real me.
The mess is peeled off
layer by layer
because I've lived,
because it shows.

Mazed

Meandering through your words
slaloming in the spaces between
I get lost and don't want to be found.

Walk

The stones I walk on are old and worn out,
thousands of feet have gone by here in time
moving away from events or towards

running or strolling, children's, old people's,
so many feet have been going this road
so many people have been where I am,
I feel one of them, on with my life now
I walk by, one in the crowd, that walks on.

Detail

In the sound of the morning coffee cup
touching the wood of the table, I find
the tune of the day. Today will be light.

Heron

The quietness that is not mine at all,
has posted on a rooftop in the street
taking a resting heron as its shape.
The bird is watching with me, the moment
when our world turns into apricot.
He is not out of place, he is a part.
The contours of the bird in marron paint
have made the light start in a better way,
now I can understand his silence well.

Molecule of the Night

Each morning when day pierces through curtains
I recollect myself to be person,
from shattered fragments all over the place
my body and my mind are being reshaped.
I return in the world of the living,
recognizing others, going through same
kinds of restoration, feel of regret.
We work our ploughs and catch our fish to eat
until day is over and sun goes down.
Every evening I fall into pieces,
to be a lost molecule of the night.

Dead

I woke up and I was dead
almost buried in my grave
with the coffin lid ajar
I could see all that was gone
and it made me feel at peace
once they closed the lid for good
I knew I'd miss nothing much

It's Just Water

I have spent too many hours
near a sea that is just water,
cried an ocean over lovers
who would never care about me
and the sea seemed there to comfort,
with a soothing sound and rhythm.

Every tear that fell, was honest
as my love had been so real then.
I have spent too many hours
near an ocean that's just water,
thinking that the sea would feel me
but it doesn't. It's just water.

Going Out the Door

The worried oak shakes his head over me;
I can't wait for him to have leaves again,
I need to see how my geese are doing,
hope to find you standing in the distance,
or someone like you. I need to feel my blood.
At home in heated rooms I can't find life
where only caged birds live. I walk in cold,
exist in memories of warmer days.
I have been dead too long now to give up.
Like trees I shall invent myself once more.

Meaningless Thoughts

Meaningless thoughts came on dancing
as I tried to do meaningful stuff.
Questions arose with no need of an answer,
they popped up in the middle of laundry.
For dreamers reality isn't enough.
At times I must be in the twilight zone of reason,
in words hiding behind the books on the shelf,
where impossible makes sense and all can be,
where you can find me as the one to hold on to
and in the meantime the laundry washes itself.

After the Birth

After the birth
of my youngest son
I hallucinated,
I saw him die in my arms
and I couldn't tell
whether I was asleep
and dreaming or in reality.

Awful memories
of my youth
melted with demons
from my mind.
After some time of fear and madness,
I was taken by lifeboat
to the mainland,

to be in a hospital ward
where everyone
was more or less crazy.

A woman would lie
in the corridor screaming,
someone was afraid
to walk outside,
another had voices in his head.
There was a woman
always knitting,
but she was staff.
(It took me a week
to figure out
who was nurse
and who was patient.
I am still not too sure
about some.)

In those sixteen days
spent there
I learnt more
about the human mind
than I did
in the rest of my life.
When I got home,
my psychosis was gone
and I now knew of the pain of others.

Forget

When words can't say horror
and no painting can draw,
no music has the notes
and nobody listens anyway,
what to do with such memories,
they come to pester in dreams
just when you know you forgot them.
Maybe bury them in the kitchen drawers
is a good idea, as those get stuck anyway
and never need to be opened again.

Let Me Wonder Them

In the heart of the flower rose
may be the end of my journey,
the reason for poems and prose
is just waiting there to be found.

Why we live, and why we die,
what follows up when all is over,
the rose must know and doesn't lie,
she promises the secret truth.

Should I open up the rose now
and find all answers lying there?
If I do, will it tell me how
I can make such a rose myself?

I'll leave the rose alone to grow,
her lovely petals stay intact.
I do not really want to know
the reasons. Let me wonder them.

Eternity in a Wave

A wave that breaks, is not yet broken,
in time it will return to sea.
A bird that dies, is not forgotten,
its flight is seen and lingers in the mind.
The wave that brought the dead bird to the shore
is not yet dead, but lives eternally.

The Crows of My Battlefield

The crows of my old battlefields
come out each night to find
remaining flesh and blood,
the eyes of whom is left behind.
They want fresh prey, new meat.
The wind is howling round the fort,
they fly low over smoke of dying fires.
They pick in wounds. They scratch in eyes.
Last night, deserted now, the battlefields
shone silver under moon and cobalt sky.
The crows took what they could, away,
and cawed some sort of a goodbye.

This morning as I woke, on my pillow lay
a feather, it was black,
the window moving in the wind, and silence.
But they'll return, they will be back.

Dire Options

In between my decision to get started
and the weather, stands a forecast, and it's bad.
More rain, could be hail, storm, and perhaps thin snow.
In between my need to go outdoors and harsh reality
sits my problem's verity on cushions by the fire.
I shall either starve or freeze. All options now are dire.

Concealing Me

Skin around blood and bones can't conceal
my blush, covering up for my mistakes, my shame.
Skin around blood and bones only hold
together what was me, before I knew you
and now is just blood and bones with skin.

In My Name

Never become numb for love,
never think that it has been enough.
When your loins ache and your heart is powder:

scream more, scream louder.
let rocks be scattered by the way you came,
and every time you do, let it be in my name.

Me in the Now

The calm of this room, from where I'm watching the storm
in light of white silver, clouds are bending their form.
They're flying, no sound, from morning till noon—
the room in deep winter when darkness comes soon.
And all is silent indoors. Peace for the making.
I do not feel much need for sound now, just taking
it in, this moment.
Not what has been, no thoughts, no how,
don't intervene. Just the room and me in the Now.

The Nights Are
Thin Cheap Walls

The nights are thin cheap walls now, erected
between reality and life. They stand,
although not well constructed. To me
they are the fence before sobriety,
the end of one more day that was a mess.
Through cracks the cold air comes to refresh me,
and more or less renewed I rise at nine.
The walls have stood and done their job, I pray
that crazy lights not trouble me today.
It's fine. Again the nights will shelter me.

Insomnia

It's really dark outside, and night,
there seems no sense to life, no sound, as all is dead
and wears the colour black in mourning now.
But after a short while, the eyes adjust and I can see
some different tones in grey. No shapes. It is enough
for reassurance though, that life is still around somehow.
If there is sense to it or not, I should not care,
at this hour, I should sleep. Not be aware.
Still, yes I am awake and shall be till the morning glow.
There is no sense to night, and as I rise, I know exactly why.
The bed looks promising, just waiting for a chance
to prove it has a use. Sleep, oh I miss you so!

Wood Containing Paper

The words came
from paper to my mind,
my mind came to the wood containing paper
absorbing meaning of the lines,
all of them as whole,
new thoughts that gave a shiver,
and every word went through my blood,
I could not stop but
read, I sought and found
every page containing
a discovery of more,
a wood of solid sentences.
I dwelled among them,

found the flood, drank
with both my hands as cups
and nourished I slept well that night.

Never Apart

Standing with my greatest fear I watch the storm go by.
We both have known some heavy weather,
always we survived.
My greatest fear won't leave me in the quiet times,
a shade in darkest corners of the room, he waits,
on sunny days might almost disappear
but never does.
We shall grow old like this, my greatest fear and me
watching how the storms go by the window.

My Body as a Cave

My body is no cathedral,
made for worship,
but more like a cave,
all brown and orange
and black inside,
with a fire burning,
that is making shades dance
on irregular wet walls.

There, for the moment safe,
all in that one room,

occasionally unwanted guests like Pain
and Fear and Hunger
find a place for the night,
together with this waiting mother,
lover, and lonely child
that are a part of me.

Sometimes a warrior is staying,
comforted in the warmth, and fed,
resting and caressed,
but never will he stay for long.
When outside the wild cats crawl,
and wolves are howling in the snow,
my body shelters all here present,
as if being in a cave.

The Funeral of a Dead Line
(or: The Morning After the Wake)

Awoke between
yesterday's bottles,
torn calendar pages
and bread on the table,
I taste the bitter sense
of this madness
that is making money,
washed down
with coffee.
Time to work.

I Am Sat at a Table of Wood

I am sat at a table of wood
on a wooden chair,
this is the kitchen
where no one is cooking anything
and nothing reminds me of life too much.

I have my laptop and my coffee mug,
the one with the crack that is not a hair,
and here is where my story has to write itself,
while outside blackbirds, dust
and autumn clouds can fly around. I do not see them.

I need no more than the crack that is no hair.
What if it was? Whose was it? Why is it in my mug?
Of goes the mind, away
from all that's wood in my kitchen.
Stories write themselves this way.

Dark Season

I watch my life grow darker now each day
and all around me lesser world is seen,
a bitter cold and storms till it is May,
a window with no view, a misty street,
my mind that's waiting but for what indeed.

The postman lost a letter no one needs,
it's flying high above the neighbour's roof,
forgotten words that no one ever reads
as rain has washed away the ink, they're gone.
The postman sighs and struggles, moving on.

I'm not that good in seasons with no light.
If I could just fast forward a few months,
or replay summer—I would be all right,
relive a bit of magic that I found.
But such is life, to live it all year round.

Enough

Find the bench under the tree,
sit here now for a while and be quiet.
Listen to the blood running through your veins.
It is the sound of you, only heard by you.
It is your life, and you should live it,
see what your eyes find around you.
No one else is seeing this now, at this time.
Feel the rain on your face, drops curiously touching you,
the wind striking your hair.
The sun might appear, telling you of warmth.
Do you really need more to convince yourself,
this is you? Need whom you are, it is enough.

Washed Ashore for No Reason

Looking for a meaning,
I found there is no message behind the sign,
no reason for coinciding events,
as nothing can be done;
it is what we see in it,
but there is no meaning, none.
So there is no value.
Still, the red balloon I found that washed ashore,
whomever sent it flying over sea,
its purpose not revealed:
it is what I saw in it,
and what to me appealed.

My Joy

let my time be filled with smallest joy
the smell of sand and the colours of water,
sound of mist and heavy clouds floating,
let my wonder be my greatest joy

From a Distance Making Sense

I only have words
I found in this language
in which to wonder
as in new found space.

A bird's footstep in snow
my mind shaping order
making its own place
in chaos of life.
I only have words
in what's not my language,
a distance from memories
now making sense.

Thought on Sunday in a Hostile World

Can I make right
to the world what was wronged
just a little bit
just a tiny effort
then I have done
not in vain
but well?

The Good Stuff

On mornings
watching the world
over coffee
I notice an inner peace
that I call happiness
but maybe it is just
a good coffee brand.

I Need Bones

I need bones, flesh, skin, and clothes
to make me person,
but I can do without those
in the long run.
Just don't expect me
to look much better,
visually wearing
only my thoughts.
Only my name.
Only my longing for you.
You need my bones, flesh, skin, and clothes
to see me person.
That is the deal
and I deliver.

This Light Is Such That I Don't Want to Go

This light is such that I don't want to go,
and leave these trees whose whispers make me hear
the ancient stories that they seem to know
as over land a mist is spread from sea.
This mist is such that I don't want to leave,
I wait to hear the soft drops fall on soil,
like tears they do, in unseen fading grief
that can't be spoken of in other ways.
But comes the night, I need to find my road,
go back to where I never knew this rest,

to shelter there, what must be my abode
until the day emerges from its sleep.
I shall return and dwell to be at ease
where light and mist make home for thought and peace.

Still Me

The hotel's bathroom mirror tells me all.
So much I didn't know about my body.
When did this happen?
If this is true,
this living image on the wall,
and it must be, then I am not
the person whom I thought I was.
I am definitely new,
differently reflecting
in that looking-glass
and shivering.
I go outside,
with this new image in my head.
There is a different, golden light.
Strangers' eyes now recognize me
differently, but still as human
(I am somewhat relieved).
A new life is beginning.
I still am woman.
I still am me.
See me.

Company

There are moments to be alone with.
They knock on your door in the early morning
and keep you company while you drink your first coffee,
in warm sunshine,
or walk with you across a deserted beach
while the sea is silver.
They show you the beauty of the dead bird's feathers.
Those moments are friends that come and go.
Invite them more often. Make them feel welcome.

One of Those Days

Sometimes a day won't really come at all,
you saw the new light but it sticks in the curtain.
To get something done, you are numb and unable.
No weather this day, grey lingers till dusk,
no hour is set for food on the table.

What happens to days that won't come to life,
that make us believe that nothing is certain,
that stay far away from the calendar pages
and will not be mentioned in history books,
not remembered or mentioned forever, for ages?

It is in those days that lives
in seclusion, unnoticed by all that makes sense
it sits in easy chairs, waiting for the right word,
or better thoughts, taking its time as daylight won't come
and hours pass without a sound heard.

As on those days of oblivion, lines are arranged
to sentences escaped from thoughts, intense
and from the blood, the flesh, the rawer side of life
that on forlorn days comes haunting in our minds
to make the poems that will cut you like a knife.

This Morning at Five A.M.

At five the light is well enough to call it day
but also night; and like the light, I'm lost this hour.
We've been through worse, I'm feeling my age now though,
it's tearing me downwards, so tired my soul is,
so weary, alone, between past and future.
At five the light is well enough but not much day.
The yesterday's coffee cups stick on the table,
the half-closed curtains won't move in the morning breeze,
at five the material world won't let go much
and early blackbirds tell me of yesterday too.
Can I let go the well-known dark that felt safer
and trade it for newer thoughts, meaning: shall I move on?

Days of No Movement

I have days of no movement
waiting for some energy
when light seems to slow down
and my thoughts are repeating.
See the shades on the pavement
overtaking elderly

overtaking the town
now my mind is retreating.
Ships need time in a harbour
leaving early morning though
as the weather is good,
they sail away to the sea.
I find shade from the arbour
watching all the ships now go
and try to change my mood,
finding me place to be.
Clouds are running above me
changing shapes, and more and more
I'm not going places,
while everyone else is gone.
Once it all was enough, we
were here together, before.
I'll wait, as the case is
now, my wandering is done.

Back in the Alley

Through the alley I went,
because from the harbour
I could hear the music
as the band was playing.
Sunshine in other streets,
festivities elsewhere,
marching older children
but here, not yet. Silence.
This was the alley where

expectations grew as
I ran bare feet over
the bricks through the darkness.
Feeling the cold I ran
towards the waiting warmth
where the music approached
and then faded away.
I don't recall the band
nor the marching children.
All that was left for me,
empty streets, setting sun.
Thinking back I suppose
I didn't make it then
but that feel was a new:
knowing expectations!
Through dark alleys I go,
the light always waiting.
Though I wear shoes now
my feet feel the cold bricks.

Change

To leave the shades of brown and grey
you need some courage, go your way
to many colours that you may
encounter.
And when you find the joy in love
then all the red won't be enough
to emphasize you're worthy of
this other.

In evening soft the dark begins
with ink as blue and black of sins
but comes the morning light, you rinse
your body.
You've left the shades when you can give
yourself a way to find you live
while sifting colours through a sieve.
You did it.

About Life

I had babies
living inside me
like fish in a bowl
and I watched my mother die.
I know nothing about life though.
Just that it happens, comes and goes.
The bowl was a good place
but scattered to pieces
with the death of the mother.

A Nomad Needs No Mortgage

With always the chance
for an incredible encounter
I travel thoughts and go by train,
by ship, by foot, eagerly
looking for something
to keep me linger a while.

I never can stay
as I do not belong where I dwell.
Not even in my thoughts I do.
A nomad needs no mortgage,
but time may be home
for that incredible encounter.

These Eyes Won't Help Me
Anymore to See

These eyes won't help me anymore to see
what lies ahead of me, nor what has been.
For good my sight has done away with me.
Now clouds have come here so relentlessly,
I see what darkness from this day might mean.
These eyes won't help me anymore to see.
I moved around not knowing I was free,
in all my days was so much to be seen.
For good my sight has done away with me.
I once saw ships above a golden sea
and flowers, colours in a meadow's green.
These eyes won't help me anymore to see.
My eyes have left me dead, relentlessly
as cold as part of some bewitched machine.
For good my sight has done away with me.
I close them now and let the darkness be
a place awaiting death, while in between
these eyes won't help me anymore to see.
For good my sight has done away with me.

Lost in the Now

In past I dwell as I feel lost,
through lanes of memories I go
away from all that is the now.
With much, too much forgotten pain
my place is in the cellar of my mind.
I am an archivist who works
in underground and mouldy rooms
where daylight never comes to me.
I place the files on rolling shelves.
Don't try to find me, this is home awhile.

I Am Born Each Morning

I am born each morning,
forgotten is the womb
by the first daylight beam
as I open the window
to greet other newborns.
We only live a day
then night comes
sucking us back into oblivion
of soft and warm and darkness.
I am born each morning.

After Waiting

In non-revealing shades I watch the day commence
as dust now dances in the sunshine void
where yesterday I still was to believe
that you would be by nightfall, sooner, real.
The Chardonnay is sour now, and caught
in red and stingy moist that were my eyes,
those shades are changing into greys and browns,
more suitable to ordinary days.

Watching the Curtains Move

I forgot to rise that day
and watched the curtains meet the sky
then fading into shades for night
and back I went to sleep;
the light of day had gone
and I slept deep this time
the world went on without me
and now I knew it could be done

How My Mind Should Be

Could there be a sky within my mind,
then I would like there to be flying birds
that carry thoughts from place to place
before the sentences become of it,

or a meadow be my thinking space
where flowers grow for inspiration
as butterflies go in between.

The Feel

If I break,
don't pick up the pieces
without at least one good household glove,
and when you throw me in the bin
you could do it at night and
throw with force;
the noise of my shattered leftovers
won't probably be enough
to bother the neighbours
in their sleep.

Leave the Door Ajar

A day like this should always end
with someone reaching for your hand,
and knowing that you have a friend.
What shame it is to find your pain
is all that's left, here to remain
and haunt you over and again.
A friend like this might come no more
into your house, but leave the door
ajar, it can be like before.

Deep Red

I know this flower, new and precious,
will only bloom for a week or three,
but it will make me see
the beauty of living,
the fullness of red,
the meaning
that I seek.
Like a friendship
that passes through in life
to disappear again,
the flower will be gone
soon after blooming
but unseen
in the ground
I know it will have found
a place for better times.
And I shall wait
for its return.

Outside

I went outside again,
this time to think
of what is worthy
in my life, and it was all:
the stumbling, the learning,
the walk,
and the fall.

The Test

You haven't been here where the secrets hide
as this place can only be reached by air,
but no plane can land, so you will have to fly
like an eagle, to get on top of the cliff
and see for yourself, what is wrong with the picture,
why the record is broken, what lies beyond fear,
and find the colour black in deeper shades.
Can you spread your wings and are you willing to
jump?

The Shades That Have No Name

Indifferent grey was with me
those years of pain and shame,
my world in harder light
than eyes can bear.

There was no name I had for this condition,
it was one of the silent mind.
Such greyness had come over me.
I saw no brightness anymore,
no one came looking for me in this dark.

I learnt to read and write.
The silent treatment gave me thoughts,
I knew from then I had a voice,
and sharpness faded
when I let it fade.

A gift in life:
relativation.
I found the colour back from there
but kept a liking for the tender shades
that mock the grey, the shades that have no names.

That I Am

We were alone, the earth and me,
as I had found a place to be
alone, and that I was.
And the trees around me only whispered
to give me some peace and quiet,
hushing the birds.
The earth had much to tell me,
but the good friend that it was, it just listened
while I did the thinking.
And then it sank in
that this was all that mattered to me.
That I am.

One Day

One day your battles are over,
you are in peace with the world
and at ease with yourself.
When you go to bed, you can sleep.
In the morning there are no regrets
and you always find reasons to rise.

There are no skeletons hiding in the cupboards
and you don't have to worry
about what you might have done,
said, slept with during the previous night.
On this fine day there are flowers,
friends really care what is going on
—they even answer your e-mails!—
and you succeed in fixing the plumbings.
Until then, stay yourself,
fight the mood and be patient.
Battles are not won in haste.

All with No Anaesthesia

Giving birth never gave me much thought
while expecting, why think about the inevitable,
but in between contractions
I could hear the moaning
of centuries of women,
an opera of labour,
I saw them squirm,
smelt them fear,
all feeling the same impossible math
trying to solve the puzzle
of a head getting through a hole
that can't be stretched so wide
if you think of it
but it can
and time after time
children came out of me
and there was nothing to it.

To Life!

There was a wellness.
I expected nothing, except everything nice
(forever the knight in his white shining armour),
a life in the way it more or less should have been.
I expected nothing though and I never would,
the armour has rusted and is squeaking like hell.
I expected nothing from the promises made,
and got what I expected, so everything's well.
There were some whispers.
I believed in nothing, except: everyone dies
(forever the hearse passing by my front windows),
as death is the way all more or less will be.
I believed in nothing though and I never would,
my windows need cleaning and my view is with dirt.
I believed in nothing from the promises made
and got what I believed in, the whispers unheard.
There were memories.
I did forget nothing, except all the bold lies
(forgiven they are, as I now know the truth well),
it's too late anyway to look further back now.
I did forget nothing though and I never shall
as our vows we renewed and new rings have been bought.
I did forget nothing from the promises made,
and what I remember, I would never have sought.

On a Heavy Thought

This thought weighs heavily on my shoulder,
won't be discouraged, comes as he pleases,
staring at me, as one dominant cat.
I didn't invite him into my house.
He is the chip that won't leave, won't learn tricks.
When I sleep, he waits, green eyes in the dark.
But now I found a way to find peace:
Twice a day I feed him with poisoned mice.

My Poetry House

For building my thoughts
I have stumbled with bricks
too heavy for me to carry.
The words slip away,
they are made of thick muck
not much concrete, more slurry.
On a rainy day
my house
crumbles and falls in slow motion.
I shall not give up
till this language gives in
so I can construct with emotion.

When I Age

Let me dance bare feet
on the beach when I age.
When my hair is grey
let me be that way
as the sea remembers.
Wave by wave I'll swim
from the shore when I age.
When my arms are thin
let me swim away
as I shall remember.

End of Journey

Maybe not soon but one day in the future
nothing you have learnt from life will matter.
You see yourself in the mirror without
thinking of altering your face or hair
and then you will know that you have found out
what the trip was about in the first place
and you can forget why you sailed away
from those windy quays on rusty trawlers,
going past misty stations in brown trains,
as it was already there, where ever
you went, it was in yourself from day one.

Dead Days

When I think of the days of not living
I go to the place buried deep in my skin
where the shivers live, and my sense of death.
And all this with the screaming, words beyond
pain, from the hungry crows on the quay
who want to be in charge of the seagulls.
Inside of me there is a quay like that
where I can watch shiploads of thoughts enter
only to be chased away by black crows.
Weird world.

It is the quiet of the day that we hear loudly
before the television tells us that the world is burning,
and as the smoking corpses are shown in the news,
we drink our coffee thinking of silence.
Take in what the pixels show us in the paper
while we wait for the bus to arrive
we are part of a meltdown in progress
and there always is coffee at five.

I Need to Get Me Out

I need to get me out
of this contemplative mood.
So much has to be done today,
but sunlight is so different now
and clouds keep changing
right before my eyes.

Can I get away
with it and call it
poetry?

Walking On

Along my walk I stop to listen.
Suddenly I sense the joy
of life surrounding me.
A lark is singing.
Some birds fly over
sharing their bright company.
To be a part of it!
So this is all, this is my truth.
The clutter gone, the air is clean.
I walk on and tree by tree
I'm coming home.

Cold Surroundings

A layer of frost is hiding you,
cold surface waiting for the sun
and it gets even colder now.
I wait for better moments.
For now everything's on hold,
only patience needed.

Aging Mirrors

When I try to see my face
in the mirror this morning
something seems different.
A new, deep line, never noticed before.
I close my eyes for the facts.
I put on my glasses,
brush my teeth,
brush my hair,
and with every action
I feel more gravity in my awareness.
Aging is interesting,
full of surprises.
And it happens to all of us
if we are lucky. Right.
Then I open my eyes,
take another look
to get acquainted
with the new, older me.
Although I am grateful for life,
and lines don't bother me really,
I still am more glad
to realize the new line,
as if my mortality is postponed now,
is a crack in the mirror glass.

But Going There Is Life

How come in parts of happiness I live,
which sometimes hide under a lot of fears
and pop out now and then when I see well,
the meaning lies of being in this world?
If I could find a way remaining there
in peace with whom I am inside, unchanged,
then I achieved the goal I set myself.
How come I am not able to succeed
to do so on my own? I do fall back
at times into my lacking self-esteem.
It will take time, but going there is life.

Last Lines of Self-Pity

The words that linger in my mind are those
I should have long forgotten, but I chose
to keep them living where they hurt me most,
reminders of the cruelties. I host,
until I find it possible to part
with all distress that makes a bleeding heart,
the words that told me I was not worth love.

For No Reason Being Happy

for no reason
being happy
I was singing
in the shower
just like that
because I live
and bad memories
will always go away
if you let them go
for no reason
being happy
means something went
for good

And I Moved On

And I moved on
as if nothing happened
and nothing happened
as if I moved on.
But the tree knows me
and knows this will pass
as change is in the air.
There is a storm coming up.
Nothing will be the same
tomorrow.

I Carve Your Soul

I carve your soul out of the pillar's salt,
drain the sour from your blood
and smile the bitter of your heart away.
At night, when you look back, I close your eyes,
kiss you into day once more,
and carve your soul out of the pillar's salt.

Giving Shape to Reality

To give reality a shape, we construct thoughts,
but thoughts, as real as they be, can drift away,
and what is real, soon loses ground and base.
As doves, say white ones just to make it nicer, they fly
through open windows of our minds. They cannot stay.
Where do those thoughts assemble, those we forgot to keep?
They only come again, disguised in dreams,
in different colours, stories, fragments,
screaming birds that catch up in our sleep.

My Maze

I wonder in the labyrinth of past
through shaded lanes of staring facts and lies
reminding me of all who didn't last,
still frightened of the secrets in their eyes.

Life goes too fast, so say the echo's cries,
damn the weariness in all their voices,
knowing I stand between the lies,
demonic ruins of fatal choices.
In the labyrinth are useful noises
that keep me motivated for this phase.
As no brave dragon slayer rejoices,
alone I'll find the exit of my maze.

Gaps

Later the words came by
to fill in the gaps
the images had left me.

Strong words made by unknown others,
I knew now what they meant
and decided I should focus
on hating the events
rather than myself. But how?

A child cannot be wiser than a grown up
and should never be expected to be.
The images will never leave me
but come closer, an acne face
haunts me in unexpected places.
Kisses never can be right.

Don't kiss me.
Don't touch me.

The gaps in learning about love
and how to be a friend,
the biggest, darkest gap of all
I never might fill up
but I am here,
events are over;
I am not.
See me.
I am living
happily ever after
for a while.

First Marriage

Darkness makes the mind grow stronger,
you whispered unseen above my head.
Old Spice took my breath away.
You had a knife with you
that you claimed had killed a man
in Africa.

Nightmares come
when daylight shines
over the ruins of what once was decent.
I don't know you any more
or less
at all.

You left the door half-open
and my free foot kicked it
till it fell loudly in the lock.

New Knee

Now walking is an issue more than norm,
as rotting knees prevent my daily round,
no excercise can keep me well and sound,
my body lost its shape, is losing form.

I'm wrecked in ice and sea before a storm,
my hope is gone to get to safer ground,
and godforsaken I shall die, unfound;
how can I feel not bad but good and warm?

You say a new knee might just do the trick,
I must admit this sounds as if good sense,
the specialist will help, my hope returns.

Maybe one day I'll lose that wretched stick.
Although I think his skills must be immense
to make me whole—I shall not have concerns.

A Song About Life

More and more curtains were closed then,
doors seemed to jam and houses burnt down.
This was the town my life used to be:
weeds taking over the streets and the walls.

I lived in a ruin, caused by habits I had.
My view blurred by spiders, that were broken glass.
I watched others clean up but give up as well.
We all lived in hell behind curtains, withdrawn.

So I moved to a life that was better for me,
the weeds here seem flowers of beauty and grace.
I feel quite relieved I have left the old place
and I open the curtains. As now I am free.

Walking Again

Meandering through what has been
I walk inside my thought,
and now and then I do look back
but never stop or leave my track.
I am free, the kind of freedom never sought,
yet found, where I do feel the ground
under my feet now,
there when the sea brings me her sound.
I walk again. Home bound.

In Fall

In fall, I do not like this lake.
Nothing trembles in the mist, when
birds are quiet in their angst of winter:
The dead men, long forgotten,
seem to watch over the surface now.
Their bodies buried here, it sounds unfair,
as they had died at sea, in autumn storm,
why bury them in water.

The lake still weeps in fall
with blackness covering the past and all
the bitter that's buried underneath.
A distant cry breaks out over the silence,
but no one else is here, the sound won't last,
still echoes for a while.

Here I come to contemplate the past.
'Twas here somebody tried to drown me
but I was not allowed to hate,
as he was so unstable.
Instead of comfort,
I was sent back into the water.

I cannot dwell too long,
but know the drowning taste
of water now, and on misty autumn days,
I do feel fear
that makes me choke.
I feel the meaning of forsake.

Home 1

Getting out of the dream,
not quite awake, no word yet spoken,
I try to linger on for more,
but church bells ring,
and curtains move, a bird is singing,
a toilet flushed.
So now the dream forsakes me,

and I become its traitor,
it does not want me woken,
starts slipping, already grudging
as I let go.
It will take
the memory away from me
before I can remember.
Before I know my name again.

Faces

After our break up
I saw faces everywhere:
they grew and aged in clouds
and moved as shadows
through bedroom curtains,
hid in darkest corners,
popped up
in thousands of fixed clones
on wallpaper, in sunbeams,
or appeared on tree barks,
telling me smiling stories
or horror scenes, pain,
but they were not yours—
the only face I searched for.

I once did see your face:
smiling, distant, different,
changed, one in the crowd of many
indifferent faces,

soon melting with them,
disappearing. Not looking for mine.

Your face became a matter of the past.
I found my own face in the mirror.
You were a memory at last.

Beach Pole

It stood as a signpost in water,
it was written in sand.
It lingered in the air
and it was a tune in my head, loud enough
to be heard for miles.
So obvious. So logical. So beautiful.

You never noticed though,
did you? You missed
the beach pole,
walked right passed
the letters spelled with shells,
you don't breathe this air anyway
and
you never got the song.

I am a shell trapped in seaweed.
My letters washed away,
the melody gone for good.
The beach pole remains.
It is there where you'll find me.

I shall be the oyster
clinging on to the rotting wood.

Home 2

I doubt the place exists
—the ruins of a Roman house
on an island far from the world,
overgrown, a labyrinth of rooms.
When children, cats, and friends have left us,
we watch the sun set every night.
There's a piano for the ghost to play on
and an antique harp, fondled by the wind;
sometimes they play together.
We have no garden but wild flowers grow
on old fundaments. We live
from what the Romans planted
and we find to eat. Sometimes
you leave me and row ashore
returning with chocolate and wine.
When you are here more and longer
to do the stuff I can't, and me,
we watch how poppies grow, dandelions.
One day we shall take the boat out
to sea, leaving forever in a mist,
leaving no trace—
I doubt the place exists.

Just Another Morning

The window open while you make coffee,
I smell the flowers. This is the season
they grow everywhere.
Syringas, you whispered earlier, pansies,
hyacinths, lilies of the valley.
(Hyacinths? Do we still have them?)

They have names, surely,
but I don't care to call them anything
as they all are: this morning,
a blend of sweet and friendly.
I imagine a rose, that would be nice,
with the coffee cup you bring.

When I put my glasses on, however,
I see it is not coffee and no rose
but a new dustpan. Hint, you smile.
It's time to rise. Almost noon.
I close the window to lock
the memory and the scents away.

The day has begun
hours before me,
already weary and troubled
but I'll catch up soon.

Before Departure

All departures are a start,
but I don't want to go into the new.
I've grown accustomed to this view
and leaving it will break my heart.

How does one part with memories
of childhood days? They seem to follow me
in streets. The chestnut trees
were always there, I watched them grow.

All starts are a departure,
familiar sights will fade in time,
I'm looking forward to a new adventure
but I don't want to lose this view.

Apostrophe

An apostrophe is all that stands between
the me and life, reality and verb,
a little dot and tail, both so superb,
connecting me to being, that I've been.

Perhaps another punctuation mark
would be a much worse chaperone for me,
as I am troubled by the verb "to be"
that chases me in daylight and in dark.

Attached so well, it's almost making one,
the "I" and "am," the I'm to be the me,
a syllable where once we had the two.

My life does know by now of how it's done,
just make a little dot, a tail and see:
I am connected to the word to be.

Thanks Maestro!

The day started differently
as I heard a piano,
to be more specific:
someone was making music
and the notes entered my room,
staccato, hammering.

As they chained together
echoing all that I felt,
they made me realize
not all was lost,
and everything
beginning.

Carry Less and Travel Light

Could we be strangers, ships that meet at night,
and see some lights ahead, in storms and rains,
not knowing whom shall pass our way, what freight
is carried? Or we might be sharing trains.

What do we know from where we come, what sight
is yours on normal days? I fear in planes
more of the people next to me than height,
what is it that they carry down inside?

Could we be strangers, as we never met?
Am I to recognise you as you are,
or are you in disguise and should I guess?

It all will be revealed when time is set,
and when we meet, please take me very far,
my stranger, let me make you carry less.

Damaged Daisy Chains

I started myself over
and made a daisy chain,
connecting every beauty
that came into my life,
with, in between white petals,
the green there to remind me
I'm a part of Earth and started
to be so at my birth.
The chain then broke quite easily,
the petals died too soon,
my labour was in vain,
again I felt mortality
nibbling at my skin.
But daisies grow forever
and show up when it's time.

I started myself over
and made a daisy chain.

Home 3

I feel at home
in a smile and a whisper,
who cares about furniture
or interior design,
this could be anywhere
but it is being near you.
You are my home,
I shall be a good tenant,
paying rent gladly
whenever it's due.

Confused

After I asked you where you would like to go,
there was some kind of confusion I'm afraid,
which had everything to do with your answer,
the description of that place.

I am so sorry for my funny behaviour,
more to the fact: that I slapped you in the face
but I didn't realize that "down under"
is a geographic phrase.

Say Once You're Free

Say once a river carried fallen wood—
a branch, ripped off a tree in summer storm,
where birds had made a nest to stay in warm,
their offspring left to spread their wings for good—
what could the branch remember of its past?

Say once that river took the wood to sea,
where tide and waves move slowly, then move fast,
to take the branch away and towards me,
would I think of the birds or former nest?
For me the branch is timber at its best.

Say once you made a promise to a lover,
the gift in silk, and joined by tasty sweet,
a ring tossed in to make more of the offer,
but she then threw you out and in the street,
would she be in your thought after a decade?

Say once you were a free man with no wife,
would you still owe to her? While she betrayed?
You can move on to make more of your life.
Here is the timber, you can build a boat,
and I'll be there to see it go afloat.

After the Funeral

Already all is silent and the grave alone.
We shall not come here often, maybe never.
The earth has taken body and the coffin, both.
Now we walk far away from here,
as rain starts falling.

A blackbird lands between the leaning stones
to take a bit of ribbon from the flowers.
A nest is built above the grave, and eggs soon come.
They have a home that's decorated with the silk,
and then eggs open.

The letters of the ribbon say: "Goodbye, dear, till eternity."
Five little blackbirds eat the worms their parents catch.
At times they sing above the grave to thank the one
deep in the ground where sound can't come. He feeds
them well, forever.

Not Set in Stone

The echos and shadows we created,
the unforseen extras of our being,
where do they go, in nights, behind our backs?
They won't give us a clue, they don't leave tracks.

Our written thoughts, our footsteps, what we say,
seem useless and forgotten very soon,
which probably is how it should be too.
New thoughts take over, so what can we do?

The echos and shadows we created,
not set in stone but lingering a bit,
they only were a part of us, a past
and we should well accept they do not last.

Memory Knows

Some times go slower than other times move,
the old man in the supermarket row
is falling forever,
I have watched my mother die too slowly in pain,
I heard my newborns cry through thick walls
and forgot the sound of their cries very soon
like I forgot the face of death but in my nightmares.
Time seems neutral, but I know that memory
is never a true reflection, I can remember
your face though.
The old man may have lived on, my mother did not
feel her own death coming perhaps.
You won't return and I shall not forget you,
some times are slower than truth, and my memory knows.

Truth

So this is all, this is my truth,
the clutter gone, the air is clean.
I walk on touching tree by tree,
I'm coming home.

Pilgrimage

About to crash
yet I know I'm stronger,
about to give in,
still I won't.
I am still moving further on.

Never the one
to obey authority,
the guide already dead and gone,
I shall go my own way,
the path meandering.

What do I mean to others,
what am I to myself,
which path to explore first?
I take some detours, not
in a hurry to find my destination.

Over misty cliffs,
through deserts,
down the deep,
that's the route
I plan to go.

About to crash
and lost at times,
so lost at times,
but never
bending for my fears.

On parallel roads the others
move into the same direction,
this voyage takes us through landscapes
we never knew about.

The flower's there
where no one seeks her,
meeting me
where nothing grows
but faith that I can make it.

The place is called
the lost horizon,
that's where I'll be
if I achieve
to be myself in darker moments.

ACKNOWLEDGMENTS

A very special thank you to the inspiration for my writings in English, David Agnew. He is a retired psychiatry nurse, a talented writer and artist, and a dear friend.

Follow his blog: belfastdavid.wordpress.com

ABOUT THE AUTHOR

Ina Schroders-Zeeders was born in the Netherlands, on the beautiful tourist-destination island of Terschelling. Her fascination with the sea began at an early age as she and her mother would frequently accompany her Merchant-Marine-Captain father on his adventures. Ina has spent her whole life enjoying books of all kinds, staying involved with libraries and book sales, until finally becoming a novelist in the late nineties. She remains on Terschelling with her husband and three sons.

Follow Ina:
inaweblogisback.wordpress.com
facebook.com/ina.schroderszeeders

www.ingramcontent.com/pod-product-compliance
Lightning Source LLC
Chambersburg PA
CBHW021925040426
42448CB00008B/914